Structure & Speaking Practice
Tokyo

NATIONAL GEOGRAPHIC
L E A R N I N G

Australia • Brazil • Mexico • Singapore • United Kingdom • United States

National Geographic Learning,
a Cengage Company

Structure & Speaking Practice, Tokyo

James R. Morgan and Nancy Douglas

Publisher: Sherrise Roehr

Executive Editor: Laura LeDréan

Managing Editor: Jennifer Monaghan

Digital Implementation Manager,
Irene Boixareu

Senior Media Researcher: Leila Hishmeh

Director of Global Marketing: Ian Martin

Regional Sales and National Account
Manager: Andrew O'Shea

Content Project Manager: Ruth Moore

Senior Designer: Lisa Trager

Manufacturing Planner: Mary Beth
Hennebury

Composition: Lumina Datamatics

Student Edition: Structure & Speaking Practice, Tokyo
ISBN-13: 978-0-357-13793-2

National Geographic Learning
20 Channel Center Street
Boston, MA 02210
USA

Locate your local office at **international.cengage.com/region**

Visit National Geographic Learning online at **ELTNGL.com**
Visit our corporate website at **www.cengage.com**

Printed in China
Print Number: 02   Print Year: 2019

Photo Credits

SCOPE & SEQUENCE

Unit / Lesson	Video	Vocabulary	Listening

UNIT 1 MY LIFE p. 2

LESSON A
People

LESSON B
Lessons learned

Inside Afghanistan's First Boarding School for Girls

People I know
classmate, coworker, friend

Taking a class
have practice, take lessons, taking a class

How do you know each other?
Listen for gist
Listen for details
Exemplify

Class and practice
Make and check predictions
Listen for gist
Listen for details

UNIT 2 LET'S EAT! p. 16

LESSON A
Foods we like

LESSON B
Eating well

Frozen, Fresh, or Canned?

Snack foods
delicious, sweet, spicy

Healthy eating habits
diet, benefits, lifestyle

Regional dishes
Make predictions
Check predictions
Listen for details

The Slow Food Movement
Make predictions
Check predictions
Listen for details

UNIT 3 MYSTERIES p. 30

LESSON A
You're in luck!

LESSON B
Unsolved mysteries

The Luckiest Unlucky Man to Ever Live

Luck
lucky, good / bad luck, chance

Why do we dream?
explanation, investigating, proof

Luck
Listen for gist
Make predictions; Listen for details

Full moon fever
Make predictions
Use visual aids; Listen for details
Listen for a speaker's opinion

UNIT 4 TRENDS p. 44

LESSON A
Lifestyle trends

LESSON B
Fashion trends

Are You Typical?

Student trends in the United States
about, exactly, increase

Fashion trends
casual, comfortable, retro, stylish

Boomerang kids
Infer information
Make and check predictions
Listen for details

Personal style
Use background knowledge
Listen for gist
Listen for a speaker's opinion

Expansion Activities p. 58

Grammar	Pronunciation	Speaking	Reading	Writing	Communication
The simple present tense vs. the present continuous tense Review of the simple past tense	Question stress	Introducing a person to someone else / Responding to introductions	Try, try again! Understand the main idea Read for details Summarize Synthesize information	Write about something you learned	Guessing classmates' identities based on their habits Talking about high school
The comparative form of adjectives The superlative form of adjectives	Sentence stress and rhythm	Making suggestions / Responding to suggestions	The healthiest lifestyle in the world? Skim for the main idea Make predictions Check predictions Scan for details	Write a restaurant review	Describing changes to a restaurant Creating a menu for a new restaurant and making plans to go out to eat
Stative verbs Modals of present possibility	Dropped syllables	Talking about possibility	Mysterious artwork Make predictions Scan for details Identify main ideas Read for details	Do research and write about an issue	Talking about intuition Describing an explanation to a mystery
Quantity expressions Giving advice with *could, should, ought to,* and *had better*	Unstressed *of*	Disagreeing / Disagreeing more strongly	Trendspotting Make predictions Check predictions Read for gist Sentence insertion Understand paraphrases	Give fashion advice to someone looking for a job	Making decisions and stating opinions Taking a fashion quiz and giving adice

Language Summaries p. 66　　　**Grammar Notes p. 68**

1 MY LIFE

A college student in Baghdad, Iraq rides a motorcycle with his friends.

Look at the photo. Answer the questions.

1 What is the man doing?

2 How do you think the men in the photo know each other?

3 Does this activity look fun to you? Why or why not?

UNIT GOALS

1 Talk about the important people in your life

2 Introduce a person to someone else

3 Talk about classes and lessons you're taking

4 Describe something you learned to do

Shabana Basij-Rasikh talks
with students at her school.

1 **VIDEO** Inside Afghanistan's First Boarding School for Girls

A Read the sentences and answer the questions.

Shabana Basij-Rasikh is an educator at SOLA (the School of Leadership,
Afghanistan). It is the first girl's boarding school in Afghanistan.

Word Bank
educator = a teacher
leader = a person who inspires and manages other people

1. What is a boarding school? (Use your dictionary to find out.)

2. Would you like to go to a boarding school? Why or why not?

B ▶ Read the sentences before you watch. Then watch the video about SOLA. Complete
the sentences with the missing words.

1. When Shabana Basij-Rasikh was young, there were no _____ for _____.

2. _____ percent of women in Afghanistan have a college degree.

3. Shabana needed to become an _____.

4. She is the _____ and cofounder of SOLA.

5. At SOLA, they create a _____ space for girls.

6. The girls come to SOLA to learn to become future _____.

7. When you educate a girl, you educate her _____ and the world.

C Get into small groups and check your answers from **B**. What do you think of SOLA? Discuss.

2 VOCABULARY

A Read about the people in Mario's life. Complete the sentences with a word for each person.

> acquaintance   classmate   coworker / colleague
> friend   girlfriend / boyfriend   neighbor

Word Bank

Word Partnerships

We're **good** / **close** / **best** / **old** friends.

They're my **next-door** neighbors.

We're **just** acquaintances.

Jason is Mario's _____.

We're best friends. We met when we were in elementary school.

Lei is Mario's _____.

We both attended the same school last year. We met and started going out.

Hakim is a(n) _____ **of Mario's.**

We met once at a party, but I don't know him well. He seems like a nice guy.

Emma is Mario's _____.

We go to the same college and have two classes together this year.

Julia is a(n) _____ **of Mario's.**

We work together in the same office, but in different departments.

David is Mario's _____.

We live on the same street.

My name is **Mario**. I'm a student at City College. I also work part time in an office.

B Look at the words in blue and think of people in your life. On a piece of paper, write *People I Know* at the top of the page. List five people and write a sentence or two about each one.

C 🔁 Tell your partner about the people in your life.

> Sergio is my friend. We met in class last year.

3 LISTENING

A 🔊 **Pronunciation: Question stress.** Listen and repeat. **Track 1**

1. A: Is he your <u>boyfriend</u>?

   B: No, we're just friends.

2. A: Is <u>your</u> boyfriend?

   B: No, he's going out with Maria.

3. A: Is <u>he</u> your boyfriend?

   B: No, <u>he</u> is.

B 🔊 **Pronunciation: Question stress.** Say these three sentences and responses.
Then listen for the stressed word in each sentence. Choose the best answer (a or b). **Track 2**

1. Are you a student at City College?

   a. No, I work there.

   b. No, I go to Essex College.

2. I thought you were her classmate.

   a. No, my brother is.

   b. No, we go to different schools.

3. I think his best friend lives next door, right?

   a. No, I think it's his colleague.

   b. No, I think he lives down the street.

C 🔊 **Listen for gist.** Listen to the conversations and number the pictures in the order (1, 2, 3) you
hear them. **Track 3**

D 🔊 **Listen for details.** Read the sentences about each conversation. Then listen again and circle the
correct answers. **Track 3**

1. a. They are / aren't dating now.

   b. They are / aren't friends now.

2. a. They are / aren't friends.

   b. They know / don't know each other well.

3. a. They know / don't know each other.

   b. They are / aren't classmates now.

E 👥 **Exemplify.** Look at your answers in **D**. Choose one of the situations and create a short dialog
with a partner. Perform it for another pair.

4 SPEAKING

A 🔊 Listen to the conversations. Which one is more informal? In each conversation, who is meeting for the first time? **Track 4**

Conversation 1

MARIA: Hi, Junko.

JUNKO: Hi, Maria. It's good to see you again! How are you?

MARIA: Fine. How about you?

JUNKO: Pretty good.

MARIA: Oh, and this is my friend Ricardo. We both go to City University.

JUNKO: Hey, Ricardo. Nice to meet you.

RICARDO: Yeah, you too.

Conversation 2

MR. OTANI: Morning, Miriam.

MIRIAM: Good morning, Mr. Otani. Oh, Mr. Otani, I'd like you to meet Andres Garcia. He started working here yesterday. Andres, Mr. Otani is our V.P. of Sales.

MR. OTANI: Nice to meet you, Andres.

ANDRES: It's very nice to meet you, too, Mr. Otani.

B What does Maria say to introduce Ricardo? What does Miriam say to introduce Andres? Underline your answers. Then practice the conversations in a group of three.

SPEAKING STRATEGY

C Work in groups of three. Follow the steps below.

1. **Student A:** Choose a famous person to be. Write down your identity on a piece of paper and give it to Student B.

2. **Student B:** Read the identity of Student A. Then introduce Student A to Student C formally. Use the Useful Expressions to help you.

3. **Student C:** Respond to the introduction.

4. Change roles and follow steps 1 and 2 again.

D Now introduce the "famous friends" you met in **C** to your other classmates. Use a formal or informal style.

> Ana, I'd like you to meet Li.

> It's nice to meet you, Ana.

Useful Expressions		
	Introducing a person to someone else	**Responding to introductions**
formal ↑	Mr. Otani, I'd like to introduce you to Andres.	It's (very) nice to meet you. (It's) nice / good to meet you, too.
	Mr. Otani, I'd like you to meet Andres.	
↓ informal	Junko, this is Ricardo. Junko, meet Ricardo. Junko, Ricardo.	Nice / Good to meet you. You, too.
Speaking tip		
When you forget someone's name, it's best to be direct and say *I'm sorry, I'm terrible with names,* or *I'm sorry, I've forgotten your name.*		

5 GRAMMAR

A Turn to page 68. Complete the exercises. Then do **B–D** below.

The Simple Present Tense vs. the Present Continuous Tense	
I always **take** a shower in the morning. She's **taking** a shower. Can she call you back?	Use the simple present to talk about habits, schedules, and facts. Use the present continuous to talk about actions that are happening right now.
I **live** in Taipei. (my permanent home) At the moment, I'm **living** in Taipei. (my home for now)	The present continuous can show that a situation is more temporary.
How many classes **are** you **taking** <u>this term</u>?	Use the present continuous to talk about actions happening in the extended present (nowadays).

B Read the sentences below. Circle the simple present tense verbs and underline the present continuous tense verbs. Then match each sentence to its usage on the right.

1. Sophia (is) my classmate.   a. describing a routine

2. She's living at home this term.   b. stating a truth or fact

3. She comes to school every day at 8:00.   c. happening right now

4. She's majoring in science.   d. happening in the extended present (nowadays)

5. We're studying together for a test right now.   e. suggesting a temporary situation

C Complete the sentences to make questions in the simple present or the present continuous. Use the verbs in the box.

do eat have ~~study~~ take talk

1. A: Why _are you studying_ English now?

   B: I need it for work.

2. A: _____ any other classes this term?

   B: Yes, I am. Two business classes.

3. A: When _____ breakfast?

   B: Around 7:00, usually.

4. A: How many brothers and sisters _____?

   B: Four brothers and one sister.

5. A: What _____ on the weekends?

   B: I relax and hang out with friends.

6. A: Who _____ to right now?

   B: Alex.

D Now take turns asking and answering the questions in **C** with a partner.

Harvard University

> Why are you studying English now?

> Well, I'm taking the TOEFL soon. I want to apply to Harvard University in the United States.

6 COMMUNICATION

A Take a sheet of paper and cut it into five strips.

On strips 1–3, write the following:

1. a routine you never change
2. an unusual habit
3. a general fact about yourself

On strips 4 and 5, write the following:

4. an activity you are doing these days
5. why you are studying English

B Give your papers to your instructor. He or she will mix up the papers and give you five new sentences.

1. I always get up at 5 AM.

2. I sometimes eat peanut butter and tomato sandwiches.

3. I have a twin brother.

4. I'm learning to play the guitar.

5. I'm studying English because it's my major.

C Talk to your classmates. Ask questions to find out who wrote each sentence.

D Tell the class an interesting fact you learned about one of your classmates.

1 VOCABULARY

A 🔄 Match a statement (1, 2, or 3) with a person above. Then ask a partner: What is each person doing? Why?

1. "I **have** track **practice** every day after school. I also **take** tennis **lessons** on the weekend."

2. "I'm **taking a class** to **prepare** for the university entrance **exam**. The class **meets** for three hours a day. It's a lot of work, but I need help to **pass** the test."

3. "Last term, I **failed** science. Now a **tutor** comes and helps me with my homework. This term, I'm **getting** a good **grade** in my science class!"

B 🔄 Complete the sentences with the blue words in **A**. Then check answers with a partner.

1. I can't go out with you. I _____ baseball _____ this afternoon.

2. Tyler never studies, so now he is _____ a bad _____ in all of his classes.

3. If I study really hard, I know I can _____ the test!

4. This term, I'm _____ two business classes at City University.

5. Our English class _____ on Tuesdays and Thursdays.

6. To _____ for tomorrow's class, please read pages 20 to 45.

7. My piano _____ aren't long. They're only 30 minutes.

8. Liam _____ his math class, so he has to retake it next term.

9. Nico is a _____. He helps students with their homework.

10. The _____ is this week, so I need to study.

Word Bank
Word Partnerships
have baseball / soccer / swim **practice**
take music / tennis **lessons**
take a(n) class / exam

C 🔄 Ask a partner the questions.

1. What classes are you taking now? When do they meet?

2. Are you taking any music or sports lessons?

3. How are you doing in your classes? Are you getting good grades?

2 LISTENING

a. He has practice in the morning only.

b. The camp lasts for a week.

c. At night, he stays in a dorm.

a. The class meets two times a week.

b. Students can work with a tutor.

c. The class is expensive.

a. The class is at a school in Singapore.

b. The class meets every day for four weeks.

c. Her teacher is Japanese.

A Make predictions. Look at the photos. Guess: What do people learn to do in each place?

B 🔊 Listen for gist; Check predictions. You will hear three people talking. Listen and number the pictures in the order you hear them (1, 2, or 3). **Track 5**

C 🔊 Listen for details. Listen again. Below each photo, circle the answer that is not true. Then correct it. **Track 5**

D 🔊 Listen for details. What are the benefits (good things) of taking each class? Listen again and write your answers below. **Track 5**

1. Her score _____ 50 points.

2. She will know how to _____ beautiful cakes.

3. He will be a _____ next year.

E 🔄 Would you like to take any of these classes? Tell a partner.

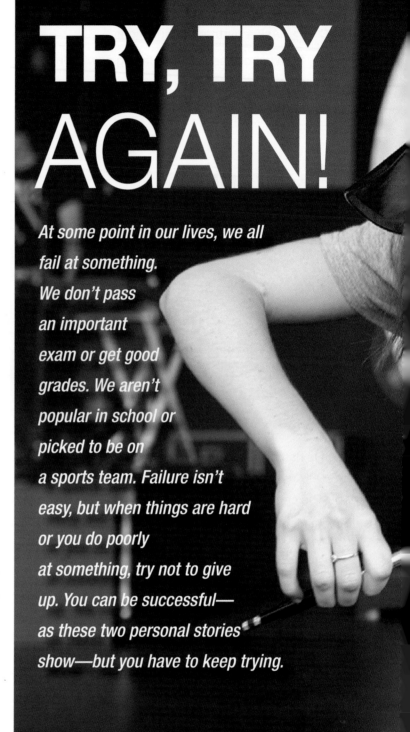

3 READING 🔊 Track 6

A Understand the main idea. Look at the words in the Word Bank. Then read the title and text below it. What is the main idea?

Word Bank
Opposites
fail (*v.*) ↔ succeed (*v.*)
failure (*n.*) ↔ success (*n.*)
successful (*adj.*)
give up (quit) ↔ keep trying

a. Sometimes it's best to give up.

b. When you fail, don't give up.

c. Careful people don't fail.

d. Some successful people give up.

B 🔁 **Read for details.** Work with a partner. Read about your person only. Then answer the questions below about him or her.

STUDENT A: Read about Black.

STUDENT B: Read about Lindsey Stirling.

1. What is the person's job?

2. What difficult things happened to the person?

3. What finally happened to the person? Was he or she successful?

C 🔁 **Summarize.** Ask your partner the questions in **B** about his or her person.

Listen and take notes. Then read about the other person. Check your partner's answers.

D 🔁 **Synthesize information.** Work with a partner. Answer the questions.

1. Look at the reading title. It is part of the expression *If at first you don't succeed, try, try again.* What does this expression mean? How are Black's and Lindsey Stirling's experiences an example of this expression?

2. Talk about a time you failed at something. When it happened, did you give up or keep trying? Did you learn anything?

TRY, TRY AGAIN!

At some point in our lives, we all fail at something. We don't pass an important exam or get good grades. We aren't popular in school or picked to be on a sports team. Failure isn't easy, but when things are hard or you do poorly at something, try not to give up. You can be successful— as these two personal stories show—but you have to keep trying.

Black is a Japanese performance artist. Today he is a successful entertainer,[1] but as a teenager, his life was very different. In school, he was quiet and shy, and other boys bullied[2] him. People said to him, "Play a sport!" but Black wasn't good at sports. Then one day, Black bought a yo-yo and his life changed. At first, he couldn't do any tricks, but he didn't give up. He watched videos and practiced. In time, he became very good, and he decided to prepare for the World Yo-Yo Contest.[3] For four years, Black worked hard and practiced. Then, at age 18, he entered the contest, and he won. On that day, he was no longer a shy high school student. He was a world champion.[3]

Lindsey Stirling is an American musician. She mixes classical violin with dance music and hip-hop. As a child, Lindsey learned to play the violin. Her parents didn't have a lot of money, so she could only take lessons part time. Despite this, Lindsey practiced a lot, and she became very good. In high school, she started writing her own songs. Then at age 23, Lindsey was on a popular TV talent show. She did well, but in the end, she lost. The judges said she wasn't interesting enough. Lindsey was very sad, but she didn't give up. She kept trying. In time, she made a music video and her first album. Later, she won an important music award. Today, she has one of the most popular channels on YouTube.

[1]An *entertainer* is someone like an actor, musician, dancer, or singer.
[2]If someone *bullies* you, they try to hurt you or make you afraid.
[3]A *contest* is a game that people try to win. The winner is the *champion*.

4 GRAMMAR

A Turn to pages 69-70. Complete the exercises. Then do **B–D** below.

Review of the Simple Past Tense		
	Yes / No questions	**Answers**
With be	Were you in class today?	Yes, I was. / No, I wasn't.
With other verbs	Did you pass the test?	Yes, I did. / No, I didn't.
	Wh- questions	**Answers**
With be	Where were you last night?	(I was) at my friend's house.
With other verbs	When did you meet your girlfriend?	(We met) last year.

calligraphy

Steve Jobs

B Complete the profile with the simple past tense form of the verbs in parentheses. Then take turns reading the profile aloud with a partner.

Apple cofounder Steve Jobs (1. not graduate) _____ from college. Jobs (2. be) _____ a smart guy, but his school (3. be) _____ expensive, and he (4. not have) _____ enough money to go. So he (5. leave) _____ college, and he (6. take) _____ a calligraphy class instead.

When his parents (7. hear) _____ this, they (8. be) _____ worried. "Why calligraphy?" his parents (9. ask) _____. "What can you do with that?" Jobs (10. not be) _____ sure. The class (11. not help) _____ him get a job, but years later, it (12. help) _____ him in another way. Jobs (13. use) _____ ideas from his calligraphy class to create Apple's famous computer fonts.

C Work with a partner. Follow the steps below.

1. On your own, write three *Yes / No* and three *Wh-* simple past tense questions about Jobs on a piece of paper.
2. Cover the profile in **B**.
3. Take turns asking and answering the questions with a partner.

> Did Steve Jobs graduate from college?

> No, he didn't.

> Why not?

D Think of a famous person from the past. Your partner asks you five past tense questions and tries to guess the person. Then switch roles and repeat.

5 WRITING

When I was fourteen, I couldn't swim. As a child, I was afraid of the water, so I never learned. Usually, this wasn't a problem, but in the summer, things were different. All of my friends went to the public pool on hot days. I went, too, but I had to watch them have fun. Finally, I decided to take swimming lessons at a place near my house. The class met every day. At first, I was very nervous, but I didn't give up. I practiced and, by the end, I was a good swimmer.

I couldn't... well, but I learned to.
dance
drive
play a sport
play an instrument
ride a bike
speak a language
speak in public
my idea: _____

A Read the paragraph. Then answer the questions with a partner.

1. What couldn't the person do?
2. Why was this a problem?
3. How did the person learn?
4. Was the person successful?

B Think about something you couldn't do, but learned to do. Answer the questions in **A** about yourself. Then use your ideas and the example above to help you write your own paragraph. Remember to use the correct simple past tense verbs.

C Exchange papers with a partner. Circle any mistakes in your partner's paper. Answer the questions in **A** about your partner. Are your experiences similar or different?

6 COMMUNICATION

A Work in a small group. Read the questions below. Then add one simple past tense *Yes / No* question and one simple past tense *Wh-* question.

In high school...

1. were you a good or bad student?
2. did you play any sports?
3. what was your favorite subject?
4. what did you do for fun?
5. _____
6. _____

B Think about your answers to the questions in **A**. Make some notes.

C Get into a group of four people. Follow the steps below.

> I was a good student in high school. I got good grades and...

1. One person begins. Choose a question in **A**.

   Speaker: Answer the question. Talk for one minute without stopping.

   Listeners: Listen to the speaker. Then answer the questions below. If the group answers *yes* to both questions, the speaker gets a point.

   • Did the speaker keep talking for one minute without stopping a lot?

   • Could you understand the person clearly?

2. Repeat step 1 with a different speaker. Continue taking turns for 25 minutes. The winner: the person with the most points.

2 LET'S EAT!

Look at the photo. Answer the questions.

1 What food is in the photo? Do you like it?

2 Is this food healthy or not? Why?

3 What are three of your favorite foods? Why do you like them?

UNIT GOALS

1 Describe foods and how they are prepared

2 Make and respond to suggestions

3 Describe a healthy diet and lifestyle

4 Rate a restaurant and explain why you like it

A man presents ice cream at an ice cream shop in Buenos Aires, Argentina.

1 VIDEO Frozen, Fresh, or Canned?

A Look at these words that describe food. Use your dictionary to look up any you don't know. Which kind of food is the healthiest to eat? Tell a partner.

fresh *frozen* *canned*

Word Bank

farmers' market = a place where local farmers sell their products directly to the public

pick = to break a fruit or vegetable off a plant or tree and collect it

salt = white powder used to improve the taste of food

B Watch the beginning of the video with the sound off. What kind of food do you see? Check (✓) your answers.

☐ fresh food ☐ frozen food ☐ canned food

C Watch again. Write one or two words to complete each sentence.

1. Frozen and canned vegetables are ________ you, too, because most are packed (put in bags and cans) right after picking.
2. But beware (be careful) of the ________ in ________ veggies.
3. ________ overboil vegetables.

D How often do you eat fresh fruit and vegetables? How about frozen or canned ones? Tell a partner.

2 VOCABULARY

A Read about a snack food called *paletas*. Find two words that mean the food is good and circle them. Would you like to try this food? Why or why not?

Paletas are **delicious**, **frozen** fruit snacks.

Their name comes from *palo* or "stick."

They are made with water or juice and fresh fruit, so they are **sweet**.

Sometimes chili pepper is added, so they can be **spicy**, too.

These **tasty** treats are a popular street food in Mexico.

paletas

B Think of a popular street food. Make notes. Use words from the Word Bank below.

Name of the food: _____

Taste: _____

Preparation: _____

> ℹ️ You can add *y* to many nouns to make adjectives meaning "full of (something)."
> **juicy   oily   salty   spicy   tasty**

a banh mi sandwich

C 🔄 Tell a partner about your food. Use your notes from **B**.

> Banh mi sandwiches are tasty. My favorite kind is made with grilled pork, cucumbers, and carrots. They are a popular street food in Vietnam.

Word Bank
How foods taste
spicy ↔ mild
sweet ↔ sour / bitter
delicious / tasty / yummy ↔ awful / terrible
How foods are prepared
baked, fried, frozen, grilled

3 LISTENING

A 🔁 **Make predictions.** Look at the four photos below. What do you think each food tastes like? Tell your partner.

B 🔊 **Check predictions.** Listen to the beginning of Bill and Marta's conversation. Complete the information about the food. **Track 7**

Foods from the (1.) _____ United States

grits

(3.) _____ green tomatoes

(2.) _____ chicken

(4.) Mississippi _____ pie

C 🔊 **Listen for details.** Listen to the rest of the conversation. Write the words used to describe the foods. Then circle the food above that Marta *didn't* like. Why didn't she like it? **Track 8**

1. The chicken was _____.

2. The grits tasted like oatmeal with a strong _____ flavor.

3. The tomatoes were _____, but they went _____ with the chicken and grits.

4. The dessert was a thick _____ pie. It was too _____.

D 🔁 Talk with a partner. Do these four foods sound good to you? Why or why not? Is your hometown (or region) famous for a special food? Describe it.

E 🔊 **Pronunciation: Sentence stress and rhythm.** Read these complaints. Then say the sentences. Underline the stressed syllables or words in each sentence. Then listen and check your answers. **Track 9**

1. The dinner was cold.

2. The chicken was dry.

3. The grits were terrible.

4. The lemon pie was too sour.

4 SPEAKING

A 🔊 Listen to the conversation. Then answer the questions.
Track 10

1. What are Jose and Jill going to eat for dinner?

2. How do Jose and Jill make and respond to suggestions? Underline the words.

JOSE: So, Jill, where do you want to go to dinner tonight?

JILL: I don't know. Why don't we go to the pizza place on the corner?

JOSE: Pizza again? I don't really feel like it.

JILL: OK, how about Thai food instead?

JOSE: Fine with me. Where do you want to go?

JILL: Well, Thai House is near here. And there's another place—The Thai Cafe—but it's downtown.

JOSE: Thai House is closer. Let's go there.

JILL: Sounds good!

B 🔄 Practice the conversation with a partner.

SPEAKING STRATEGY

C 🔄 Study the Useful Expressions. Then complete the dialogs below with a partner. Sometimes more than one answer is possible.

1. A: _____ stop at that cafe for coffee.
   B: Good _____!

2. A: What time do you want to meet in the morning?
   B: _____ meet at 7:00?
   A: That's a little early. _____ meeting at 8:00 instead?
   B: That's _____ with me. See you then.

3. A: What do you want to do today?
   B: _____ going to the beach?
   A: I don't _____ to. _____ see a movie instead.
   B: OK, _____ good.

Useful Expressions			
Making suggestions			**Responding to suggestions**
Statements			Good / Great idea!
Let's	have	Thai food for dinner.	(That) sounds good (to me).
Questions			(That's) fine with me.
Why don't we	have	Thai food for dinner?	I don't really want to.
How about	having		I don't really feel like it.
Speaking tip			
When rejecting a suggestion, it's common to give an explanation: *I don't really feel like it. I'm too tired.*			

Why don't we go to Parr's Steakhouse for lunch?

That's a great idea!

I don't really feel like steak. How about having Indian food instead?

D 👥 Get into a group of three and do the following:

1. On your own: think of two good restaurants.

2. Suggest one of the restaurants to your partners. They can accept or refuse. If a person refuses, he or she should say why and suggest another restaurant.

3. Change roles and repeat steps 1 and 2 until each student makes a suggestion.

5 GRAMMAR

A Turn to pages 70–71. Complete the exercises. Then do **B** and **C** below.

The Comparative Form of Adjectives			
One syllable	**Two syllables**	**Three or more syllables**	**Irregular forms**
old → old**er**	quiet → quiet**er**	comfortable → **more** comfortable	good → **better**
nice → nic**er**	spicy → spic**ier**		bad → **worse**
big → big**ger**	famous → **more** famous		

Note: The comparative form of *well* (an adverb) is *better*.

B Use the words to make questions with *which* in the comparative form.

1. tasty / restaurant food / your own cooking

   Which is tastier, restaurant food or your own cooking?
   _____

2. go well with steak / french fries / a baked potato

   _____

3. good / drinking tea / drinking coffee

   _____

4. fun / eating out with family / getting fast food with friends

   _____

5. bad / arriving 30 minutes early to a dinner party / being 30 minutes late

   _____

> **i** We typically use *which*, not *what*, when there is a smaller, more defined number of choices.
> *What did you have for dessert last night?*
> *Which pie did you bake for the party, the chocolate one or the lemon one?*

C 🔄 Ask and answer the questions in **B** with a partner. Give reasons for your answers.

> Which is tastier, restaurant food or your own cooking?

> My own cooking is tastier. I'm a pretty good cook!

6 COMMUNICATION

A Look at the pictures of Veronica's Restaurant. Talk with a partner about the changes you see. Use the adjectives in the box to help you.

bad	comfortable	new
bright	dirty	nice
busy	good	old
cheerful	messy	sad
clean		

the old Veronica's

the new Veronica's

> The old Veronica's was dirty.
> The new Veronica's is cleaner.

B With a partner, make a twenty-second radio advertisement for the new Veronica's using your ideas from **A**. Write your ideas below. Then practice the announcement aloud.

_____

_____

_____

_____

C Present your radio advertisement to the class. Whose was the best? Why?

> Come and see the new Veronica's!
> It's brighter and better than ever.

Mexico, Japan, Cameroon, and Greece. How are these countries similar? In her book *The Jungle Effect*, Dr. Daphne Miller says these places have some of the world's healthiest people. Why? Their traditional diets have important health benefits, says Dr. Miller. The things they eat and drink increase their energy and protect them from dangerous illnesses.

Dr. Miller says a healthy diet and lifestyle are important. She says we should:

- eat more fresh fruit, vegetables, and fish.
- cut back on red meat and instant (pre-made) foods. Only eat these sometimes.
- completely eliminate unhealthy habits like smoking.
- get plenty (lots) of exercise.

a table of traditional Greek food

1 VOCABULARY

A 🔁 Read the information above. Then answer the questions with a partner.

1. How are the four countries mentioned similar? Why are their traditional diets special?
2. Would Dr. Miller agree with these statements? Why or why not?

   Eat more hamburgers.   *Don't smoke at all.*   *Going to the gym once a month is enough.*

B Take the quiz. Circle T for *True* and F for *False*. Choose the answers that are true for you.

1. I need to cut back on red meat in my diet.   T   F
2. I eat plenty of fruit and vegetables.   T   F
3. I get plenty of exercise.   T   F
4. I have one or two bad habits.   T   F

C 🔁 Do you have a healthy diet and lifestyle? Why or why not? Use your answers in **B** to tell a partner.

> I have a healthy diet and lifestyle.
> I get plenty of exercise, and I eat...

2 LISTENING

Tadka dal, a spicy traditional **dish** (food) from India, has many health benefits.

Today, more people worldwide eat **fast food**, and health problems are increasing.

A Look at the photos. Which is healthier: tadka dal or fast food?

B 🔄 **Make predictions.** You will hear two people talking about the Slow Food Movement. Guess: Which idea(s) (a–d) do its members believe are true? Circle the idea(s). Explain your guesses to a partner.

People should _____.

a. not eat fast or instant foods

b. grow food slowly and carefully

c. not eat meat

d. learn to cook their own meals

Word Bank
movement = a group of people with the same beliefs
member = part of a group

C 🔊 **Check predictions.** Listen and check the correct answer(s) in **B**. **Track 11**

D 🔊 **Listen for details.** Read the sentences. Then listen again and circle *True* or *False*. **Track 11**

Alessandro Moretti thinks…

1. most Slow Food members are Italian.	True	False
2. eating a slow food diet is hard for busy people.	True	False
3. a slow food diet has health benefits.	True	False
4. many people today don't know how to cook.	True	False
5. you should learn your grandparents' recipes.	True	False

E 🔄 Discuss the questions with a partner.

1. Do you like the Slow Food Movement's ideas? Why or why not?

2. Do you eat a lot of fast food? Can you cook any traditional dishes?

3 READING 🔊 Track 12

THE HEALTHIEST **LIFESTYLE** IN THE WORLD?

A 🔁 **Skim for the main idea; Make predictions.** Look quickly at the title, picture, and article. Then try to guess the correct answers below. Explain your ideas to a partner.

1. The reading is mainly about _____.

   a. people from around the world

   b. healthcare for older people

   c. a group of people from Japan

   d. older people in the United States

2. What is unusual about these people?

   a. Most of them are women.

   b. Many live to age 100 or older.

   c. They have the spiciest food in the world.

   d. There are only 100 of them.

B **Check predictions.** Now read the article and check your answers in **A**.

C **Scan for information.** Read quickly through the article again and complete the chart below. You have two minutes.

Okinawan Centenarians

What they eat	What they drink
_____	_____
_____	_____
_____	How they relax
_____	_____
How they exercise	_____
_____	_____
_____	_____

D 🔁 Answer the questions with a partner.

1. Why do Okinawans live so long? Give reasons from the reading.

2. Do people in your country have healthy lifestyles? Use the chart in **C** to give examples.

An 84-year-old Okinawan man does yoga daily on the beach in Naha.

In many countries around the world, people are living longer than before. People have healthier lifestyles, and healthcare is better, too.

Okinawa is an island off the coast of Japan. The people on Okinawa, the Okinawans, may have the longest lives and healthiest lifestyles in the world.

Researchers did a study. They started by looking at city and town birth records from 1879. They didn't expect to find many centenarians (hundred-year-olds) in the records, so they were very surprised to find so many old and healthy people living in Okinawa. The United States, for example, has ten centenarians per 100,000 people. In Okinawa, there are 34 centenarians per 100,000 people!

What is the Okinawans' secret? First, they eat a healthy diet that includes fresh fruits and vegetables. They also eat fish and tofu and drink plenty of water and green tea. But researchers think that the Okinawans have other healthy habits as well. They don't do hard exercise such as weightlifting or jogging. Instead, they prefer relaxing activities like gardening and walking. They sit quietly and relax their minds by breathing deeply. They also spend time with family members and friends.

4 GRAMMAR

A Turn to pages 71–72. Complete the exercises. Then do **B–D** below.

The Superlative Form of Adjectives			
One syllable	**Two syllables**	**Three or more syllables**	**Irregular forms**
old → **the** old**est**	quiet → **the** quiet**est**	comfortable → **the most** comfortable	good → **the best**
large → **the** large**st**	spicy → **the** spic**iest**	important → **the most** important	bad → **the worst**
big → **the** big**gest**	famous → **the most** famous	relaxing → **the most** relaxing	

B Complete the restaurant profile with the superlative form of the adjectives in parentheses.

Are you looking for an interesting place to have a meal? One of (1. unusual) _____ places in

the world is Ithaa Restaurant in the Maldives, where you eat underwater! Ithaa is one of

(2. trendy) _____ restaurants in the world. For many, it is also (3. popular) _____

place to visit in the Maldives. It's not (4. cheap) _____ restaurant, but it's

(5. good) _____ way to see the island's coral and fish. The food is good, too. "I had

(6. delicious) _____ meal of my life," says one visitor to the restaurant. His girlfriend agrees.

"It was (7. weird) _____ but (8. interesting) _____ dining experience I ever had!"

C 🗩 Answer the questions with a partner.

1. Why is the restaurant in **B** unusual?

2. Why do people like it?

3. Does it sound interesting to you? Why or why not?

bad	cheap	romantic
boring	noisy	trendy

D 🗩 Work with a partner. Use the adjectives in the box to talk about restaurants and cafes you know.

> The Left Bank is the noisiest cafe in this area.

5 WRITING

Amazon Sun

Amazon Sun is the best Brazilian restaurant in this city. The food is delicious, the service is friendly, and the prices are moderate. One of the tastiest dishes on the menu is the feijoada completa—a traditional dish of meat, beans, and Brazilian spices. It's excellent!

A Read the restaurant review and complete the notes about the place. Then ask and answer questions about the restaurant with a partner.

Restaurant name: _____

Type of food: _____

Prices: expensive / moderate / cheap

Service: _____

Best dish: _____

> Is it an expensive restaurant?

> No, the prices are moderate.

B Choose a restaurant you know and make some notes about it. Use the model in **A**. Then use your notes to write your own restaurant review.

C Exchange your writing with a partner. Read his or her review.

1. Are there any mistakes? If yes, circle them.

2. Complete the notes in **A** about your partner's place.

3. Give the review back to your partner. Do you want to try his or her restaurant? Why?

6 COMMUNICATION

A With a partner, create a menu for a new restaurant or coffee shop. Divide the menu into sections (appetizers, main dishes, drinks, desserts). Include prices.

B Post your menus for the class to see. Then walk around and learn about the restaurants in your class. Take notes.

C Work with your partner. Answer the questions about the restaurants in your class.

1. Which restaurant is the cheapest?   3. Which has the healthiest food?

2. Which is the most expensive?   4. Which is the best? Why?

> Why don't we try Noodle Barn?

> Sounds good. I love ramen!

D Choose a restaurant from the class list. Suggest eating there with your partner. Use the Useful Expressions on page 21.

3 MYSTERIES

Look at the photo. Answer the questions.

1 What is unusual about the tree in the photo?

2 Can scientists explain this mystery?

3 What other mystery do you know about? Can science explain it?

UNIT GOALS

1 Say how likely something is

2 Talk about states and feelings

3 Say if something is possible or impossible

4 Explain a mystery

African baobab trees can live to be thousands of years old. Scientists still don't understand why some trees live so long.

Frane Selak's car plunged off of a mountain road, but he survived!

1 **VIDEO** The Luckiest Unlucky Man to Ever Live

| lucky |
| unlucky |
| survived |
| accidents |

A Frane Selak is called the "luckiest unlucky man to ever live." Complete the information about Frane with the words in the box.

Frane had many _____. That was _____. But he _____. That was _____.

B ▶ Read the question and answers on the left. Watch the video. Then put the events in order from 1 to 7.

What unlucky things happened to Frane?

_____ His car went off a mountain road.

_____ He was in a plane crash.

_____ He was in a bus crash.

__1__ He was in a train crash.

_____ His car burst into flames.

_____ A bus hit him.

_____ His car burst into flames—again.

Why was he lucky?

a. A door blew off, and Frane landed in a haystack.

b. Frane only broke his arm.

c. Frane jumped free.

d. Four people were killed but not Frane.

e. Frane survived.

f. Frane jumped out and landed in a tree.

g. Frane survived (but with less hair).

C ▶ Why was Frane lucky each time? Watch again. Match each event (1–7) with a reason (a–g).

D 🔁 Answer the questions with a partner.

1. What lucky thing happened to Frane in 2003?

2. Why is Frane the luckiest unlucky man to ever live? Explain in your own words.

2 VOCABULARY

A Answer the questions.

1. **Lucky** people have good things happen to them. Are you lucky? Why or why not? _____
   _____

2. Do you ever do things (like wear a lucky color) for **good luck**? Do you do anything to avoid **bad luck**? _____
   _____

3. Write down some notes about something good that has happened to you. Did you do it **on purpose** (plan it), or did it happen by **chance** (by luck)? _____
   _____

4. Do you make decisions based more on **facts** (true information about something) or on your **intuition** (feelings)? Explain. _____
   _____

5. What lucky objects do you know about? Do you own a lucky object? Where do you keep it? How does it help? _____
   _____

6. *It's better to be lucky than to be smart*. Do you agree or disagree with this statement? Why? _____
   _____

Word Bank
Opposites
lucky ↔ unlucky
good luck ↔ bad luck
(do something) on purpose ↔ (happen) by chance
facts ↔ intuition

B 🔄 Ask and answer the questions in **A** with a partner.

> Do you do anything to avoid bad luck?

> People say that stepping on a crack in the sidewalk is bad luck, so I don't do it.

Some people think that seeing a rainbow is a lucky sign.

3 LISTENING

A 🔊 **Pronunciation: Dropped syllables.** Say these words. Look up any words that you don't know. Then listen and repeat. **Track 13**

1. interesting   2. generally   3. everywhere   4. finally

B 🔄 Read the sentences. Which one do you agree with more? Tell a partner.

1. Some people are just lucky in life.   2. You can learn to be lucky in life.

C 🔊 **Listen for gist.** You will hear a talk about psychologist Professor Wiseman and his research on luck. Listen. Which sentence in **B** (1 or 2) does he believe? Circle it. **Track 14**

D 🔊 **Make predictions; Listen for details.** Read the statements below. Do they describe lucky people or unlucky people? Make predictions. Then listen and check your answers. **Track 15**

Write *L* for "lucky people." Write *U* for "unlucky people."

Write *B* if it is true for <u>both</u> types of people.

1. _____ They spend more time alone.
2. _____ They don't like surprises.
3. _____ They have a lot of friends.
4. _____ They make decisions.
5. _____ They follow their intuition.
6. _____ They have bad experiences.
7. _____ They try to find the good in a bad situation.

> ### Word Bank
> Sometimes, words have different meanings depending on how they are used.
>
> ***take a chance***   *chance* = risk
>
> ***by chance***   *chance* = luck
>
> ***increase your chances***
> *chances* = opportunities

ℹ️ Notice as you listen: The speaker uses *on the other hand* to introduce a contrasting (or an opposite) idea.

E 🔄 Answer the questions with a partner.

1. Was your answer in **B** the same as Professor Wiseman's? Do you agree with him? Why or why not?
2. Look at the statements in **D**. Which ones are true for you?

Many cultures have lucky charms. The *maneki-neko* is popular in Japan.

4 SPEAKING

A 🔊 Nico and Sandra are talking about a news article. Listen and answer the questions. **Track 16**

1. What did a woman in New York City do?

2. What is she going to do now?

SANDRA: Anything interesting in today's news?

NICO: Yeah, I'm reading about a woman in New York City. She just won $25,000.

SANDRA: That's a lot of money. Did she win the lottery?

NICO: No, she guessed the correct number of candies in a jar.

SANDRA: Really? How many were there?

NICO: 7,954.

SANDRA: Wow. That was a lucky guess!

NICO: I know. I doubt that I could do that!

SANDRA: So, what's she going to do with the money?

NICO: I don't know. Perhaps she'll go on a vacation or use it for school.

B 🔄 Practice the conversation with a partner.

SPEAKING STRATEGY

C On the lines below, write two things about yourself that are true. Write one thing that is a lie.

_____

_____

_____

How many candies are in this jar?

Useful Expressions: Talking about Possibility	
Saying something is likely	
I bet (that)	Marco plays the drums.
Marco probably	plays the drums.
Maybe / Perhaps	Marco plays the drums.
Saying something is *not* likely	
I doubt (that)	Marco plays the drums.
Speaking tip	
You can use *Are you sure?* to ask if a person is certain about something.	

D 👥 Get into a group of three or four people. Follow the steps below.

1. One person tells the group his or her sentences.

2. The others...

   • ask the speaker questions to find out which sentence is a lie.

   • use the Useful Expressions to discuss their ideas.

   • guess which sentence is a lie. If you guess correctly, you get a point.

3. Change roles and repeat steps 1 and 2.

> I bet **Marco** plays the drums. I saw him with a pair of drumsticks one time.

> Are you sure they were his drumsticks? Maybe they belong to someone else.

5 GRAMMAR

A Turn to pages 72–73. Complete the exercise. Then do **B–D** below.

Stative Verbs				
Thinking verbs	**Having verbs**	**Feeling verbs**	**Sensing verbs**	**Other verbs**
believe		appreciate		seem
know	have	_____	see	look
_____	_____	_____	_____	mean
_____		love	taste	cost
				need

B Look at the stative verbs in the box below. Then add them to the chart at the top of the page.

> belong   hate   hear   like   own   smell   think   understand

C Read the story below. Circle the correct form of each verb. Use the present continuous wherever possible.

Winning the lottery—to most people, it (1.) seems / is seeming like great luck. Unfortunately, for the winners, it's often the opposite. Ian Walters, for example, won a million dollars in a lottery five years ago. "Suddenly (2.) you have / you're having a lot of money," he explains. "(3.) You think / You're thinking it will last forever, and you spend it quickly." And then one day, the money is gone. "These days, (4.) I live / I'm living with my sister temporarily, and (5.) I work / I'm working in a small cafe. (6.) I don't own / I'm not owning a car because I can't afford it," says Ian. "It's not so bad, though. I now (7.) know / am knowing that money can't buy happiness. (8.) I appreciate / I'm appreciating each day. And (9.) I look forward / I'm looking forward to the future."

> **i** Stative verbs are not usually used in the present continuous tense.

D 🔁 Answer the questions with a partner.

1. *Winning the lottery seems like good luck.* Do you agree with this statement?
2. Do you think money can buy happiness?
3. Do you need a certain amount of money to live?
4. What do you do to appreciate every day?

6 COMMUNICATION

A Read the story. Then look at the photo. Without looking back at the story, answer these questions with a partner.

1. Who is Corina Sanchez?

2. What happened to Corina at around 12:00?

3. What happened to her son at around the same time?

4. How did Corina know?

On the morning of February 19, Corina Sanchez said goodbye to her husband and 17-year-old son and went to work. "It was a normal day," Corina remembers.

She went to lunch at the usual time: 12:00. Suddenly, she started to feel terrible. "I had a strong pain in my chest—near my heart," says Corina. "The pain came and went quickly. It was very strange."

Two hours later, Corina got a phone call with some bad news. Her son was in a car accident. Luckily, he wasn't hurt badly. The time of the accident? 12:02 PM.

B Discuss the questions with a partner.

1. How did Corina know that something was wrong?

2. Some people think that mothers have special abilities. Do you believe in a "mother's intuition"?

C Think of a time when you had intuition about a situation or when something strange happened to you or someone you know. Complete the chart with your notes.

Who is the story about?	
What happened?	

D Tell your story to a partner.

Why do we dream?

Everyone dreams, but scientists can't figure out why. Below are two explanations

"Our team is investigating the connection between dreams and our health.
Dreams might help us deal with stress. After we sleep and dream, we feel better."

"We have a different theory. Maybe dreams are just images in our minds.
We dream because the brain is 'cleaning out' unused information when we sleep."

Both ideas make sense, but for now, there's no proof for either one.
The only way to solve this mystery is to do more research.

1 VOCABULARY

A 🔁 Look at the photo and the question *Why do we dream?* Think of answers with a partner.

B 🔁 Take turns reading the information above with a partner. Then match the words in blue with a definition below. Some words have the same definition.

Word or Phrase	Definition
figure out,	to find an answer to a question or problem
theory,	a guess or idea
	to study something closely
	to be logical or understandable
	facts that show that something is true

C 🔁 Answer the questions with a partner. Use your ideas from **A** to explain your answers.

1. What are the two theories about dreams?

2. Do scientists have proof for either idea?

3. In your opinion, which explanation makes more sense?

Word Bank
Word Partnerships
have / need / there's (no) **proof**
have a **theory**

2 LISTENING

Some people think that more people act in a strange or dangerous way when the moon is full.

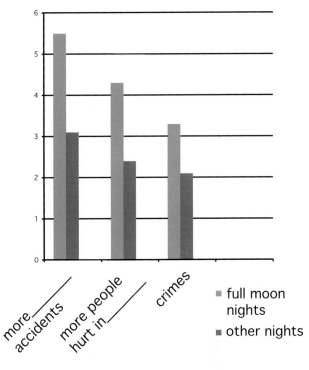

■ full moon nights

■ other nights

A 🗣 **Make predictions.** Look at the photo and the graph. Read the information. Then answer the questions with a partner.

1. What do some people think about the full moon?

2. Look at the graph. What do you think it's showing?

<table>
<tr><td colspan="2">**Word Bank**</td></tr>
<tr><td>If something *affects* you, it causes you to change in some way.

behavior = the way you act</td></tr>
</table>

B 🔊 **Use visual aids; Listen for details.** You are going to hear a news report. **Track 17**

1. Listen and complete the graph in **A**. Write one word in each blank.

2. What are city officials planning to do? Write your answer.

_____

C 🔊 **Listen for a speaker's opinion; Listen for details.** Read the questions and answers. Then listen and check (✓) *Yes* or *No* and complete the chart. **Track 18**

	Does the moon affect our behavior?	**What's the person's theory?**
The woman	☐ Yes ☐ No	The moon affects the _____. Maybe it affects _____, too.
The man	☐ Yes ☐ No	On full moon nights, there's more _____, so more people _____.

D 🗣 Answer the questions with a partner.

1. What do you think? Can the moon change our behavior?

2. Can you think of any other explanations for the higher crime and accident rates?

A **Make predictions; Scan for details.** Look at the title and photo and answer the questions below. Then look quickly though the article to check your answers.

1. What do you think the drawing in the photo is?

2. Who do you think made it?

B **Identify main ideas.** Read the passage. Then write the questions below in the correct places in the interview. Two questions are extra.

How did they make the lines?

What was the purpose of the lines?

How do the local people feel about the lines?

What exactly are the Nazca Lines?

Can anyone visit the Nazca Lines?

Who made the ground drawings?

C **Read for details.** The statements below are wrong. Change them so that they are correct. Underline the sentence(s) in the interview that helped you make your changes.

1. The lines are small; you can only see them by looking closely at the ground.

2. North Americans probably created the lines in the year 1500.

3. It was probably difficult for people to make the lines without simple tools.

4. The Nazca Lines definitely were a calendar, say scientists.

D 🗨 Look at the four questions in the interview. Take turns asking and answering them with a partner. When you answer a question, use your own words. Try not to look back at the article.

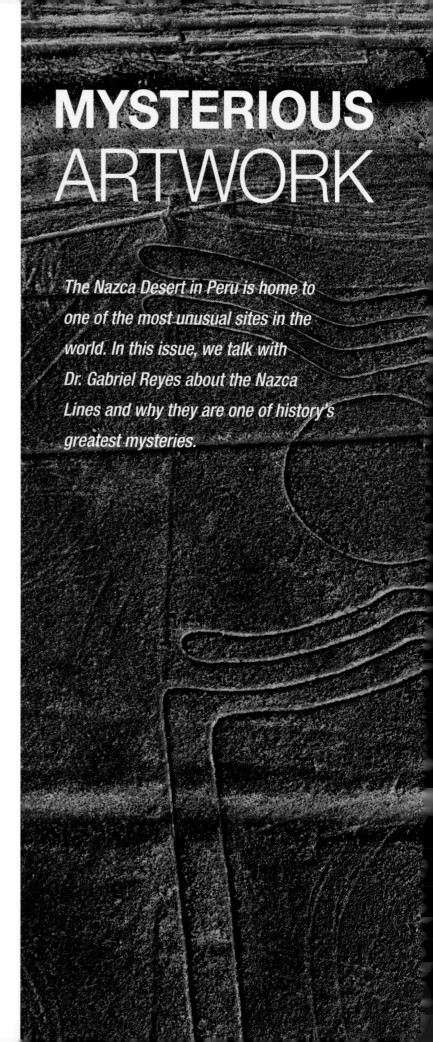

MYSTERIOUS ARTWORK

The Nazca Desert in Peru is home to one of the most unusual sites in the world. In this issue, we talk with Dr. Gabriel Reyes about the Nazca Lines and why they are one of history's greatest mysteries.

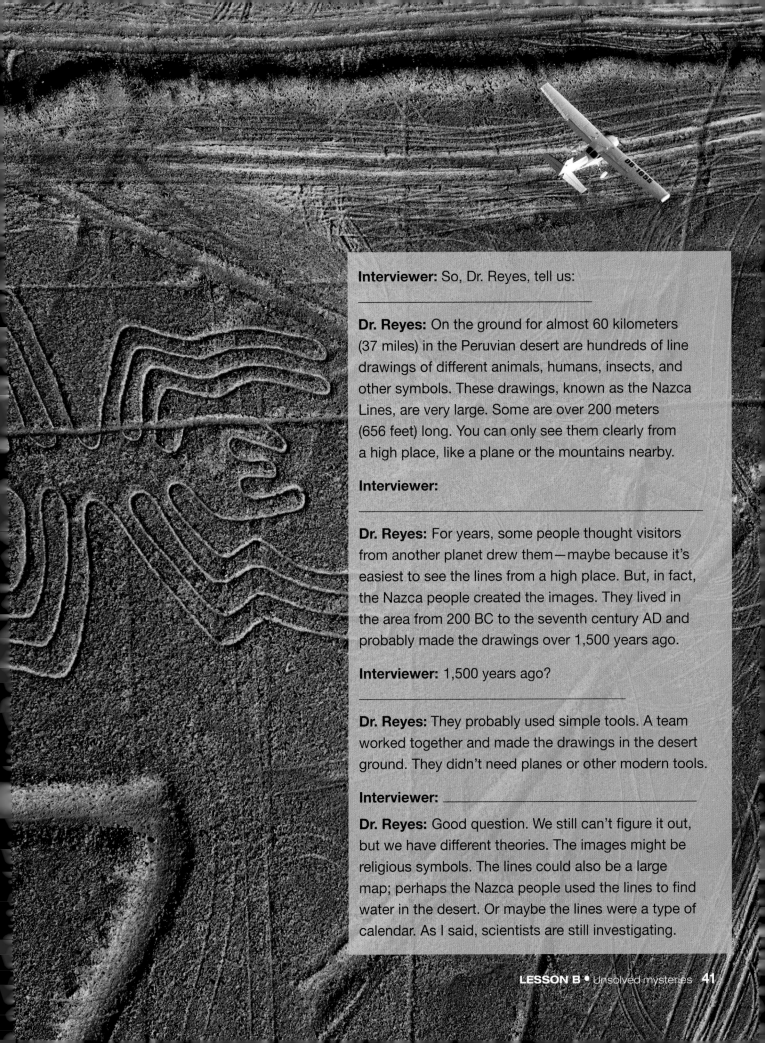

Interviewer: So, Dr. Reyes, tell us: _____

Dr. Reyes: On the ground for almost 60 kilometers (37 miles) in the Peruvian desert are hundreds of line drawings of different animals, humans, insects, and other symbols. These drawings, known as the Nazca Lines, are very large. Some are over 200 meters (656 feet) long. You can only see them clearly from a high place, like a plane or the mountains nearby.

Interviewer: _____

Dr. Reyes: For years, some people thought visitors from another planet drew them—maybe because it's easiest to see the lines from a high place. But, in fact, the Nazca people created the images. They lived in the area from 200 BC to the seventh century AD and probably made the drawings over 1,500 years ago.

Interviewer: 1,500 years ago? _____

Dr. Reyes: They probably used simple tools. A team worked together and made the drawings in the desert ground. They didn't need planes or other modern tools.

Interviewer: _____

Dr. Reyes: Good question. We still can't figure it out, but we have different theories. The images might be religious symbols. The lines could also be a large map; perhaps the Nazca people used the lines to find water in the desert. Or maybe the lines were a type of calendar. As I said, scientists are still investigating.

4 GRAMMAR

A Turn to pages 73–74. Complete the exercises. Then do **B** and **C** below.

Modals of Present Possibility			
Subject	**Modal**	**Main verb**	
The Loch Ness Monster	**may / might / could**	be	real. Maybe it's a large animal.
	can't		real. There are no sea monsters.

Questions and short answers		
With *be*	Is the Loch Ness Monster real?	It **may / might / could** be.
With other verbs	Does the full moon affect us?	It **may / might / could**.

B Complete the dialogs with a modal and a verb, if needed. Sometimes, more than one answer is possible. Then ask and answer the questions with a partner.

1. A: Does life exist on other planets?

   B: It _____. There are billions of planets. We _____ be the only intelligent life.

2. A: Worldwide, millions of bees are dying. Scientists can't figure out why. What's happening?

   B: Pesticides _____ be killing the bees. But it _____ be climate change, too.

3. A: Are ghosts real?

   B: Sure, they _____. A lot of people see them.

   C: No, they _____. There's no scientific proof for them.

Word Bank
pesticide = a chemical used to kill insects

C Ask the questions in **B** with a partner again. This time, give and explain your own opinion.

5 WRITING

A Read the paragraph. Answer the questions with a partner.

1. What question is the writer answering?

2. What is the writer's opinion? What ideas does he use to support his opinion?

B Read the question below and circle your answer. Then complete the notes. Research facts and experts' opinions to support your opinion.

> **Are ghosts real?** They might be. / They probably aren't.
> Fact(s) / Findings / Experts' opinions about this:
>
> 1.
>
> 2.

> Does life exist on other planets? It might. **Scientists think that** there are billions of planets in the universe. Some of these planets may be similar to Earth. **In fact,** scientists found hundreds of planets like Earth last year. These planets might have water, and they might not be too hot or too cold. There could be simple life forms on them. Maybe one day we will solve this mystery.

C Use your ideas in **B** and the example in **A** to write a paragraph of your own.

D 🔄 Exchange papers with a partner.

1. Circle any mistakes in your partner's writing.

2. Answer question 2 in **A** about your partner's paragraph. Do you agree with your partner?

6 COMMUNICATION

A Look at the photos and read the notes about these unsolved mysteries. What do you think each thing is? Circle your answers.

The Yonaguni Monument

What: The Yonaguni Monument is a large underwater rock formation about 25 meters (82 feet) high in the Pacific Ocean, near Japan. The mysterious objects look like the pyramids in Egypt and the Americas.

a. an underwater city

b. a pyramid built by the Egyptians

c. nothing, just some rocks

d. your idea:
_____

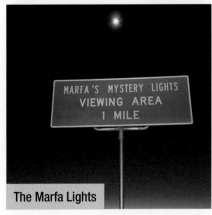

MARFA'S MYSTERY LIGHTS
VIEWING AREA
1 MILE

The Marfa Lights

What: The Marfa Lights are lights that appear suddenly in the night sky. Often, there are two or three of them. They are about the size of a basketball. Sometimes they fly close to people's houses. People first saw them in 1883 in the desert near the town of Marfa, Texas (US).

a. lights from a car or plane

b. some kind of strange weather

c. a UFO

d. your idea:
_____

B 👥 Work in a small group. Discuss each of the possible answers to the question in **A**. Which is the most likely explanation?

> The Marfa Lights might be lights from a car or plane...

> No, they can't be because...

C 👥 Can you think of another unsolved mystery like the ones in **A** or on the Grammar page? Tell your group about the mystery. They will think of explanations for it.

4TRENDS

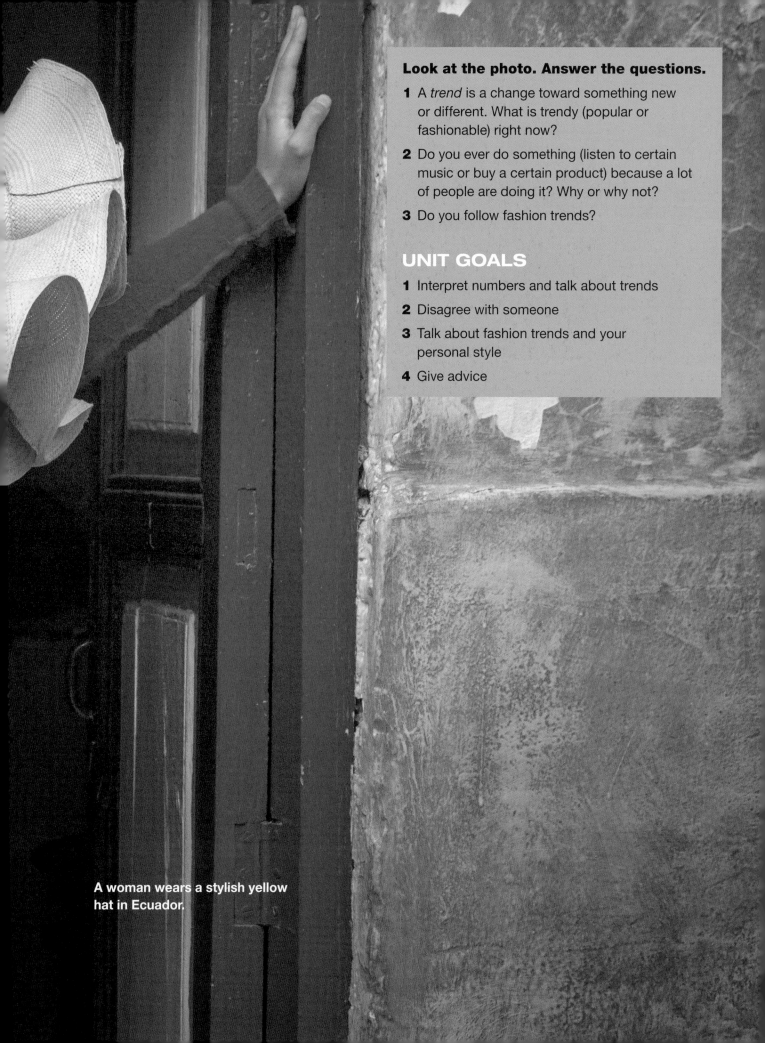

Look at the photo. Answer the questions.

1 A *trend* is a change toward something new or different. What is trendy (popular or fashionable) right now?

2 Do you ever do something (listen to certain music or buy a certain product) because a lot of people are doing it? Why or why not?

3 Do you follow fashion trends?

UNIT GOALS

1 Interpret numbers and talk about trends

2 Disagree with someone

3 Talk about fashion trends and your personal style

4 Give advice

A woman wears a stylish yellow hat in Ecuador.

There are over seven billion people in the world. What do you think the most "typical" person looks like?

1 VIDEO Are You Typical?

A Complete the sentences with information about yourself. How typical do you think you are? Discuss with a partner.

1. I am a(n) _____-year-old _____ female / male.
   (e.g., Australian, French)

2. I am right-handed / left-handed, I have / don't have a cell phone, and I have / don't have a bank account.

B ▶ You are going to watch a video about the most typical person in the world. Read sentences 1–3 and try to guess the answers. Then watch and complete the sentences.

1. The most typical person is a(n) _____-year-old _____ female / male.

2. The most typical person is right-handed / left-handed, has / doesn't have a cell phone, and has / doesn't have a bank account.

3. By 2030, the world's most typical person will come from _____.

C Discuss these questions with a partner.

1. Are you similar to the world's most typical person? Why or why not?

2. The video mentions a future change to the world's most typical person. What is it? What do you think is causing this change?

2 VOCABULARY

A 🔄 Look at the pie charts below. What do they show about student life in the United States? Tell a partner.

B 🔄 Read the sentences below each pair of pie charts. Circle the correct word to complete each sentence. Compare your answers with a partner's.

TRENDS IN AMERICAN STUDENT LIFE

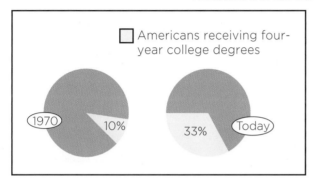

☐ Americans receiving four-year college degrees

1970 — 10%   33% — Today

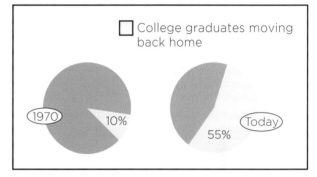

☐ College graduates moving back home

1970 — 10%   55% — Today

1. In 1970, about / exactly 10% of Americans received a four-year college degree.

2. Today that number is nearly / precisely 35%.

3. The number today is more than three times / four times as high.

4. The number of people with a college degree dropped / increased from 1970 to today.

5. In 1970, over / under 20% of college graduates moved back home to live with their parents.

6. Today, almost half / more than half of college graduates are moving back home.

7. There are more than four times / five times as many graduates moving home today.

8. The number of graduates moving back home rose / fell from 1970 to today.

C 🔄 Discuss the questions with a partner.

1. In your opinion, which trend(s) in **B** are positive? negative? Why?

2. Are these trends similar or different in your country? Explain.

3 LISTENING

A **Infer information.** Read about Alex below. What do you think the term *boomerang kid* means?

Alex is nearly 25 years old. He left home to go to college when he was 18 years old. He graduated from college over three years ago. About a year after graduation, he moved back home to live with his parents. Alex is known as a "boomerang kid."

B 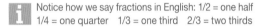 **Make predictions.** Look at the chart. Read the information about Alex's life before, his life now, and his hopes for the future. What do you think he is going to say about his life? Tell a partner.

> ℹ Notice how we say fractions in English: 1/2 = one half
> 1/4 = one quarter   1/3 = one third   2/3 = two thirds

Nearly 50% of college graduates move back home at some point.

	Before	Now	In the future
Living situation	lived in an _____	lives at _____	going to find a _____
Rent	more than _____ a month	_____	going to _____ the rent
Money	didn't have _____ of money	saves _____ of his salary	
Work	couldn't find _____	works _____	wants to find a _____ job

C 🔊 **Check predictions.** Listen to Alex talk about his life. As you listen, complete the chart in **B**. **Track 20**

D 🔊 **Listen for details.** Listen. Complete the paragraph. **Track 21**

My mother told me not to give up. But it's not so _____. When my mom was _____, she graduated from college and _____ a job pretty quickly. Now more people go to college, and there is more competition for _____. It's a lot _____.

E 🔄 Read the paragraph in **D**. Then discuss the questions below with a partner.

1. Do you think it's harder for college graduates now? Why or why not?

2. When do children typically move out of their parents' home in your country? Do they ever move back home? If so, why?

4 SPEAKING

A 🔊 🔁 Listen to the conversation. Then answer the questions with a partner. **Track 22**

1. What are Carla and her dad fighting about?
2. Who do you agree with, Carla or her dad?

CARLA: Dad, can I talk to you for a minute?

DAD: Sure, what's up?

CARLA: Well, my friend Marta is going to see a concert tomorrow night, and she invited me to go.

DAD: Tomorrow night? But tomorrow's Tuesday. Sorry, Carla, but no.

CARLA: Dad! You *never* let me do anything.

DAD: That's not true, Carla. You do lots of things. But the concert ends late, and you have school on Wednesday.

CARLA: I know what you're saying, Dad, but it's just one night. And all of my friends are going.

DAD: Sorry, Carla, but the answer is still no.

CARLA: Oh, Dad, you're so unfair!

B 🔁 Practice the conversation with a partner.

SPEAKING STRATEGY

C 🔁 Work with a partner. One person is the parent. The other person is the son or daughter.

1. Choose a situation from the box below. Think of reasons for and against it.
2. Create a new conversation similar to the one in **A**. Include at least two Useful Expressions.

D 👥 Get together with another pair.

- **Pair 1:** Perform your conversation for another pair.
- **Pair 2:** Listen. Who do you agree with—the parent or child? Why?

E 👥 Switch roles and do **D** again.

Useful Expressions	
Disagreeing	**Disagreeing more strongly**
I know what you're saying, but…	I'm afraid I disagree.
I see what you mean, but…	Sorry, but I disagree.
Yes, (that may be true), but…	That's (just) not true.
I'm not so sure about that.	I totally / completely disagree.
Speaking tip	
You can soften your disagreement by first saying that you understand the other person's point. *I see what you mean, but I still don't think it's a good idea.*	

Parents: Your son or daughter wants to…

- go on a date.
- visit another country by himself or herself.
- get a part-time job.
- your own idea: _____

5 GRAMMAR

A Turn to pages 74–75. Complete the exercises. Then do **B–D** below.

Quantity Expressions				
Quantity	*of*	**Determiner**	**Plural count noun**	
All **Most** **A lot** **Half** **Some** **None**	of	my	friends	live at home.
		Pronoun		
		them		

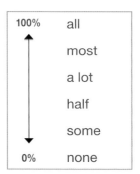

100% all
↑ most
  a lot
  half
  some
0% none

B 🔊 **Pronunciation: Unstressed *of*.** Practice saying the three sentences below. Then listen and repeat. Notice the pronunciation of the word *of* in each one. **Track 23**

1. A lot of college graduates move back home.
2. Most of my friends live at home.
3. Some of them have part-time jobs.

Word Bank
a couple = two

C Read the information about six families from around the world. Then write *all*, *most*, *a lot*, *some*, *a couple*, or *none* in the blanks below.

	The SHAW family	The IKEDA family	The OLIVEIRA family	The CHOI family	The VEGA family	The KUMAR family
Hometown	Chicago	Tokyo	São Paulo	Seoul	Mexico City	New Delhi
Language	English	Japanese	Portuguese	Korean	Spanish	English
Housing	house	apartment	apartment	apartment	house	apartment
Transportation	car	subway	bus	car	car	bus
Wife works at...	restaurant	office	hotel	office	office	office
Children	no	yes	yes	yes	yes	yes

1. _____ of the families live in big cities.
2. _____ of the families speak English.
3. _____ of them speak French.
4. _____ of the families live in apartments.
5. _____ of them own cars.
6. _____ of the wives work.
7. _____ of them work in an office.
8. _____ of the families have children.

D 🔁 Tell your partner about the families you know using *all (of)*, *most (of)*, *a lot (of)*, *half (of)*, *some (of)*, *a couple (of)*, or *none (of)*. Use the list below.

have children   speak a little English   live in the city

live in a house / apartment   own a car   have a mother who works

6 COMMUNICATION

A Read the situations below. For each one, choose the answer you agree with or write your own idea.

Luis wants to go to design school, but his father wants him to go to City University. Luis doesn't want to go there, but if he doesn't, his father will not pay for school. What should Luis do?

a. Go to City University like his father wants.

b. Start at City University and then later transfer (move) to another school.

c. Get a job, save his money, and pay for his own education.

d. Your idea: _____

Yukiko's 16-year-old brother hangs out with some bad people. He isn't going to class, and he is fighting at school. Yukiko is worried. What should she do?

a. Wait a little longer. Maybe things will change.

b. Talk to her brother. Tell him her feelings.

c. Tell her parents about her brother.

d. Your idea: _____

Josh is dating Holly. Josh loves her, but his parents don't like her. This weekend is Josh's birthday. His parents are having a party, and they have invited all his friends—except Holly. What should Josh do?

a. Talk to his parents and tell them to invite Holly.

b. Just bring Holly to the party.

c. Skip the party and spend the day with Holly.

d. Your idea: _____

B Get into a small group. Talk about your opinions in **A**. Explain the reasons for your choices.

> I think Luis should go to City University.

C Look back at each situation in **A**. How many people in your group agreed with answers a–c? How many came up with their own answers? Compare your results with another group.

> Most of our group members think Luis should go to City University.

> Really? Most of us think he should go to design school.

Fashion Flashback

What styles were in (popular) a decade ago?

1 VOCABULARY

A 🔄 Work with a partner. Look at the photos and read the question.
Then match the words (a–e) below with the clothing items in the photos.

a. **ripped** jeans   d. an **oversized** shirt

b. **baggy** shorts   e. **skinny (fitted)** jeans

c. **pointy** shoes

B 🔄 Answer the questions with a partner.

1. Are the styles above still in?

2. Which words in the box do you know?
   Which are new?

3. Which words in the box describe the styles
   in the photos? Which describe your look?

Word Bank
Describing your look (style)
casual / comfortable ↔ formal / conservative
colorful
dramatic / flashy ↔ plain / simple
elegant
retro / vintage
stylish
sporty
unique / unusual ↔ common / ordinary

2 LISTENING

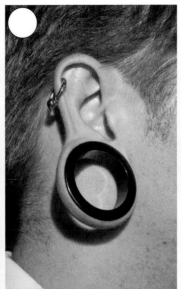

A 🔄 **Use background knowledge.** Look at the photos and answer the questions with a partner.

1. What are the people in the photos wearing?

2. What adjectives from page 52 describe each person's look?

B 🔊 **Listen for gist.** Listen. You will hear three different conversations. What are the people talking about? Number the photos (1, 2, or 3). One photo is extra. **Track 24**

C 🔊 **Listen for a speaker's opinion.** Read the sentences below. Then listen again. Circle the correct word and write one word in each blank. **Track 24**

Photo 1

1. The woman likes / dislikes the ear piercings because they're too _____.

2. The man likes / dislikes the style. He says it's a _____ look.

Photo 2

3. The man's office dress code is mostly "business _____."

4. The man likes / dislikes his office dress code. It's more _____ than the one at his last job.

Photo 3

5. The girl says her brother's look is very _____.

6. The girl likes / dislikes this style because it's _____.

D 🔄 Answer the questions with a partner.

1. Do you like the styles in the photos? Why or why not?

2. Does your school or workplace have a dress code? Explain.

3 READING 🔊 Track 25

A 🔁 **Make predictions.** Read the ad below. Then answer the questions with a partner.

1. What do you think a trendspotter does?

2. Who would hire a trendspotter?

> Are you between the ages of 15 and 22? Do you like fashion and music? Do you know what's hip?
>
> You could be a **trendspotter**!
> - Try new products!
> - Participate in surveys!
> - Receive free samples!

B **Check predictions; Read for gist.** Brooke is 18 years old. She works as a trendspotter. What does she do? Read her posts and check your answers in **A**.

C **Sentence insertion.** Write each sentence below in the correct place in the reading. One sentence is extra.

Yesterday, they were here in the studio.

I can't wait for our next meeting!

Then she gave us a tour of the studio.

There were about ten of us.

D 🔁 **Understand paraphrases.** Check (✓) the sentence(s) Brooke would say about being a trendspotter. Explain your answers to a partner.

1. _____ It's kind of boring.

2. _____ You can make good money.

3. _____ You get free things.

4. _____ You work with famous people.

5. _____ People ask your opinion about lots of things.

E 🔁 Answer the questions with a partner.

1. Why do you think companies use trendspotters? Do you think it's a good idea?

2. Would you like to be a trendspotter? Why or why not?

TRENDSPOTTING

Part-time Job

Today I started my new part-time job as a trendspotter. I was nervous and didn't know what to expect. Well, guess what? It was a lot of fun! I'm telling all of my friends, "You should think about becoming a trendspotter, too!"

This morning, we had to report to a recording studio[1] by 10 AM. The "Trends Coordinator," Mandy, explained the schedule. _____. That was really cool!

Next we sat around a big table in a room. _____. Mandy gave each person three cards. One card said "Yes—All the way!" Another said, "It's OK." The third one said, "No way!" We listened to about ten different songs. After each song, we had to hold up a card. They played some hip-hop, rock, heavy metal, and dance music. The heavy metal was "No way!" for me!

Gifted

Do you know the rock group Gifted? They're really popular right now. _____. Too bad we missed them. Anyway, they have a new album coming out soon. We saw six different album covers. (I guess they are trying to choose one.) This time, we didn't have any cards. Instead, we just talked about the covers we liked. Mandy asked us questions: "Which ones do you like?" and "Why do you like them?"

We finished at 12:30. We meet again next week at a boutique[2] downtown. We will look at some new fashions. Each week we go to a different location. Oh, and we also received a gift card for our work. This "job" doesn't pay, but we get free stuff!

That's all for now!

[1]Musicians make music in a *recording studio*.
[2]A *boutique* is a small store.

4 GRAMMAR

A Turn to page 75. Complete the exercise. Then do **B** and **C** below.

Giving Advice with *could, should, ought to,* and *had better*	
You **could** wear a dress to the party. You **could** wear the blue dress or the black one.	Use *could* to make a suggestion or give advice. It is often used to offer two or more choices.
You **should / ought to** wear a formal suit to the job interview. You **shouldn't** wear jeans. They're too casual.	Use *should* or *ought to* to give advice. Both are stronger than *could*.
You'**d better** wear a coat. It's going to rain. We'**d better not** drive to the concert. It will be hard to park.	Use *had better (not)* to give strong advice.

B 🔗 Look at the list and think of three pieces of advice to give your partner.

Student A: You are going to an informal birthday party at an American friend's home.

Student B: You are going to a formal dinner party at the British consulate.

arrive a little late	wear a suit or a nice dress	wear ripped jeans
bring food	bring a friend who wasn't invited	wear something elegant
wear casual clothes	bring flowers or a small gift to the host	wear unique clothes

C 🔗 Work with a partner. Tell your partner your plans. He or she will give you some advice and explain it.

> I'm going to a birthday party at an American friend's home. Should I bring something?

> Yeah, you could bring..., but you shouldn't...

5 WRITING

A 🔗 Read the post from Sad Sam. What is his problem? Tell a partner.

B Now write a response to Sam. Give him some advice.

C 🔗 Exchange papers with a partner.

1. Correct any mistakes in your partner's writing.

2. Do you agree with your partner's advice? Why or why not?

Ask Susie Style

Dear Susie Style,

I need your help! I can't get a job. Everywhere I go, I get the same answer: "No!" Is my appearance the problem? Here is a picture of me. What do you think? What should I do?

Sad Sam

6 COMMUNICATION

A Ask your partner the questions. Check (✓) your partner's answers.

How often do you...	often	sometimes	never
1. wear "the same old thing"?	☐	☐	☐
2. buy something because it's cheap?	☐	☐	☐
3. wear something comfortable but mismatched?	☐	☐	☐
4. wear something until it's worn out?	☐	☐	☐
5. leave the house without looking in the mirror?	☐	☐	☐
6. read fashion magazines about new trends?	☐	☐	☐
7. change your hairstyle?	☐	☐	☐
8. shop for new clothes or shoes?	☐	☐	☐

B Calculate your partner's score. Use the table.

	For questions 1–5	For questions 6–8
often	score 2 points	score 0 points
sometimes	score 1 point	score 1 point
never	score 0 points	score 2 points

Word Bank

If something is *worn out*, it is old and unusable.

If you *get a makeover*, you do things to improve your look.

C Read the appropriate advice to your partner. What does your partner think of the advice?

0–3 points: You know what's "in," and you're very stylish. Keep up the great work!	**4–7 points:** You have a good sense of style, but you could change a few things or just try to do something new every week.	**8–12 points:** Your look might be a little plain. You could change something about your clothing or hairstyle. You should also try to go out more and see what's happening.	**13–16 points:** You scored a lot of points. You'd better think about getting a complete makeover!

1 STORYBOARD

A Susan, Maya, and Bruno work together. Look at the pictures and complete the conversations. For some blanks, more than one answer is possible.

B Practice the conversations with a group of three. Then change roles and practice again.

C Role-play. Introduce a friend to another friend. Invite both friends out to dinner.

2 SEE IT AND SAY IT

A Below is a page from Anna Lopez's high school yearbook. She graduated in 2010. Read what her classmates wrote in her yearbook. How did Anna know each person? Discuss your ideas with a partner.

Sorry I didn't get to know you better, Anna. Good luck in college! Bobby

Hey, Anna! Best friends 4-ever! Rachel

Michael Evans

Bobby Leong

Anna Lopez

Rachel Williams

We're graduating, but you'll always be my girl, Anna. ~Michael

B Look below to see the people in **A** as they are today.

1. What are their relationships now?

2. Choose one of the pictures below. Make up a story about it. Answer these questions:
   - What happened to the people after high school?
   - How did they meet again?

3. Tell your partner the story of your picture.

Bobby and Anna

Rachel and Michael

3 LISTENING

A Look at the photos below. What words would you use to describe these things? Tell your partner.

B Four people are going to talk about their eating habits. Listen. Which food does each person like or eat a lot? Match a speaker (1, 2, 3, or 4) with the correct photo. **Track 26**

C Read the sentences below. Then listen. Choose the correct answer for each sentence. **Track 27**

1. If you *get in shape*, you...
   a. gain weight.
   b. do things to be healthier.
   c. don't do much exercise.

2. If food tastes *bland*, it has...
   a. a strong taste.
   b. a lot of spices in it.
   c. no flavor.

3. If you *have a sweet tooth*, you...
   a. like sugary foods.
   b. can't eat sweets.
   c. are a good cook.

D Work with a partner. Follow the steps below. **Track 26**

1. Write three more food items in the chart.

2. Listen again. Which person (1, 2, 3, or 4) probably eats the items on your list often? Check (✓) your answers.

Food or drink item	Person 1	Person 2	Person 3	Person 4
1. pizza				
2. a salad				
3. a candy bar				
4. _____				
5. _____				
6. _____				

3. Discuss your answers with a partner. Talk about the possibilities.

> I doubt that Person 1 eats pizza because...

> I don't know. He might eat it because...

E Which person (1, 2, 3, or 4) are you most like? Why? Tell your partner.

4 WONDERS OF THE WORLD

A 🔄 Use the adjectives in the box to ask and answer questions about these monuments with a partner.

beautiful	interesting	popular	strange
impressive	old	remote	tall

The Great Wall of China

The statues on Easter Island

The Eiffel Tower

The Roman Colosseum

> Which monument is the oldest?

> Well, the statues on Easter Island look old, but I think the Roman Colosseum is older.

5 I'M READING AN INTERESTING BOOK.

A Choose three words from the box. Write three sentences about yourself in your notebook. Use the simple present or the present continuous tense.

eat	know	like	own
read	study	work	

B 👥 Work in small groups. Read one of your sentences. Each person in your group asks a question about your sentence.

> I always eat cereal for breakfast.

> What kind of cereal do you eat?

> I'm reading an interesting book.

> Oh, really? What are you reading?

6 STORYBOARD

A Ruben is talking to his teacher, Gina Walker. Complete the conversations. Then tell a partner: Why does Ruben want to talk to Professor Walker?

The next day in Professor Walker's office . . .

B Practice the conversations with a partner. Then change roles and practice again.

7 SEE IT AND SAY IT

A Look at the neighborhood and discuss the questions with a partner. Take notes.

1. What are the people doing?

2. How are the people getting around?

3. How many pedestrians are there?

4. Does this look like a walkable neighborhood?

5. What places can you see in the picture?

6. What types of clothing are the people wearing?

B Tell another group about the scene.

8 I NEED YOUR ADVICE!

A Read the sentences. What advice would you give to someone who made these statements? Think about your answers.

1. I'm always late.

2. I forgot to bring today's English homework, and it's 25 percent of the class grade.

3. My parents don't like my friends.

4. It takes over two hours to get to school every day. I hate it.

5. I get really nervous when I have to talk to others in English.

6. I bought a new cell phone, and it's not working.

B Get into a group of three people. Write the numbers 1 to 6 on six small pieces of paper. Put the numbers in a bag or hat.

- When it's your turn, choose a number. Read aloud the problem in **A** that goes with your number. Explain the problem in more detail. Use your imagination.

- Your partners will listen and give you advice.

- Think about their suggestions. Which person gave you the best advice? Why?

9 BE GOING TO OR WILL?

A The chart shows the different uses of *be going to* and *will*. Complete the sentences below with *be going to* or *will*. Both may be correct in some sentences.

	To talk about plans you already made	To talk about a sudden decision	To make a general prediction about the future
be going to	✓		✓
will		✓	✓

1. Two weeks ago, I decided to take the TOEFL exam. I _____ take it next spring.

2. It's a beautiful evening. I think I _____ take a walk.

3. I bet there _____ be thousands of people at the free concert in the park tomorrow.

4. What _____ do this weekend? Do you have any plans?

5. A: The two o'clock movie is sold out, but we still have seats for the four o'clock show.
   B: OK, I _____ take two tickets for the show at 4:00.

6. She's really smart. I bet she _____ get accepted to a good school.

B Compare your answers with a partner's. Explain why you chose *be going to* or *will* in **A**.

10 LISTENING

A Read the poll below and choose your answer. Share your ideas with the class.
What was the most common answer in your class?

POLL:

Do you think you'll get married?

a. Yes, definitely. I want to get married.
b. Yes, maybe someday, but I'm not sure when.
c. No, never. Marriage isn't for me.
d. I'm already married!

B A magazine asked a group of university students for their opinions on different topics.
Listen and put the charts in the order (1–4) you hear them talked about. **Track 28**

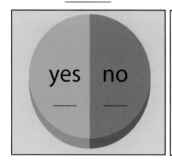  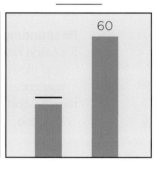 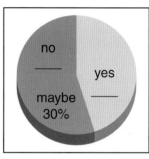

C Listen again and label the parts of each chart in **B** with the correct numbers or percentages.
Some numbers will not be given. You have to guess them. **Track 28**

D Look at your answers (1–4) in **B**. What do the students interviewed think?
Read the sentences below and then choose the correct answer.

Chart 1: Over / Under 65% of the students think it's OK for couples with children to get divorced.

Chart 2: More students think studying abroad is good. The number dropped / rose.

Chart 3: Nearly / Exactly half of them think the university entrance exam is too difficult.

Chart 4: Around / Exactly three-fourths of them answered *Yes* or *Maybe* to this question. Do you
think plastic surgery is OK?

E What do you think about the four opinions in **D**? Compare your ideas with a partner's.
Explain your reasons.

> I think it's OK for couples
> with children to get divorced.

> Really? I'm afraid
> I disagree.

UNIT **1** MY LIFE

LESSON A

Vocabulary

friend
We're good / close / best / old friends.

acquaintance
I don't know her (very) well. / She's just an acquaintance.

girlfriend / boyfriend
We're dating. / We're seeing each other. / We're going out.

coworker / colleague
We work together. / We're in the same department / office.

neighbor
We're next-door neighbors.

classmate
We're in the same class. / We go to the same school.

Speaking Strategy

Introducing a person to someone else
Mr. Otani, I'd like to introduce you to Andres.
Mr. Otani, I'd like you to meet Andres.
Junko, this is Ricardo.
Junko, meet Ricardo.
Junko, Ricardo.

Responding to introductions
It's (very) nice to meet you.
  (It's) nice / good to meet you, too.
Nice / Good to meet you.
  You, too.

LESSON B

Vocabulary

get a (good) **grade**
have (baseball, soccer) **practice**
meet
pass ↔ **fail**
prepare (for something)
take (music, swimming, tennis) **lessons**
take a (class, test) / **an exam**
tutor
win, won, winner ↔ lose, lost, loser

failure (*n.*), fail (*v.*) ↔ success (*n.*)
succeed (*v.*), successful (*adj.*)
give up (quit) ↔ keep trying

UNIT **2** LET'S EAT!

LESSON A

Vocabulary

baked
delicious / tasty / yummy ↔ **awful / terrible**
farmers' market
fried
frozen
grilled
juicy
oily
salty
spicy ↔ **mild**
sweet ↔ **sour / bitter**

Speaking Strategy

Making suggestions
Let's have Thai food for dinner.
Why don't we have Thai food for dinner?
How about having Thai food for dinner?

Responding to suggestions
Good / Great idea!
(That) sounds good (to me).
(That's) fine with me.
I don't really want to.
I don't really feel like it.

LESSON B

Vocabulary

benefit
cut back on ↔ **increase** (something)
a (healthy) **diet**
a (traditional) **dish**
eliminate
fast food
a (bad / unhealthy) **habit**
lifestyle
member
movement
plenty (of something)
protect (you from something)

UNIT 3 MYSTERIES

LESSON A

Vocabulary

lucky ↔ **unlucky**
good luck ↔ **bad luck**
(do something) on purpose ↔
  (happen) by chance
facts ↔ **intuition**

take a chance (= risk)
by chance (= luck)
increase your chances
  (= opportunities)

Speaking Strategy

Talking about possibility
Saying something is likely
I bet (that) Marco plays the
  drums.
Marco probably plays the drums.
Maybe / Perhaps Marco plays the
  drums.

Saying something is not likely
I doubt (that) Marco plays the
  drums.

LESSON B

Vocabulary

affect
behavior
explanation
figure (something) out
figure out (why something
  happens)
Experts / Scientists say / think /
  believe (that)...
In fact...
investigate
mysterious
make sense
(have / need / show / there's no)
  proof
solve (a problem / a mystery)
(have a) **theory**

UNIT 4 TRENDS

LESSON A

Vocabulary

trend

increase / rise ↔ **decrease /
  fall / drop**
over / more than ↔ **under / less
  than**

exactly / precisely
approximately / about / around
nearly / almost

a couple
one half
two thirds
percent
twice as high as...
three times as many as...
typical

Speaking Strategy

Disagreeing
I know what you're saying, but...
I see what you mean, but...
Yes, (that may be true), but...
I'm not so sure about that.

Disagreeing more strongly
I'm afraid I disagree.
Sorry, but I disagree.
That's (just) not true.
I totally / completely disagree.

LESSON B

Vocabulary

a **look** / style
(to be) in (style)

Types of clothing
baggy / oversized ↔ **fitted**
  (shirt, pants, jeans)
pointy (shoes)
ripped (jeans)
skinny

Describing personal style
casual / comfortable ↔
  formal / conservative
colorful
dramatic / flashy ↔ **plain /
  simple**
retro / vintage
stylish / elegant
sporty
unique / unusual ↔ **common /
  ordinary**

UNIT **1** MY LIFE

LESSON A

The Simple Present Tense vs. the Present Continuous Tense	
Simple present	**Present continuous**
Use the simple present to talk about habits, schedules, and facts.	Use the present continuous to talk about actions that are happening right now*.
I always **take** a shower in the morning. The express train **arrives** at 9:03 AM. They **don't speak** Italian. They **speak** French.	She**'s taking** a shower. Can she call you back? Hurry up! The train **is leaving**! Look at me! I**'m speaking** to you!
Sometimes the simple present and the present continuous have similar meanings, but use of the present continuous can show a situation is more temporary.	
I **live** in Taipei. A: Every summer, my family goes to the beach. B: Nice! **Do** you **stay** in a hotel?	At the moment, I**'m living** in Taipei. A: Let's have lunch at my hotel. B: Sounds good. Where **are** you **staying**?
	*Also use the present continuous to talk about actions happening in the extended present (nowadays). Notice the <u>time expressions</u>.
	How many classes **are** you **taking** <u>this term</u>? She **is living** in Singapore <u>these days</u>.

A Veronique Lesarg is a doctor. Use the simple present or present continuous to complete her profile.

My name (1. be) _____ Veronique Lesarg. I (2. live) _____ in Montreal.
I (3. be) _____ a pediatrician, a doctor for children. I usually (4. work) _____
in a hospital, but these days, I (5. volunteer) _____ for an organization called
Doctors Without Borders. They (6. send) _____ staff to other countries. This year,
I (7. work) _____ in Africa. At the moment, I (8. write) _____ to you from
a small village. There's no hospital here, so right now we (9. build) _____ one.

B Write two simple present and two present continuous questions about Veronique Lesarg.

1. _____   3. _____

2. _____   4. _____

LESSON B

Review of the Simple Past Tense				
Subject	**Verb**		**Time expressions**	
I You	**missed** didn't miss	a tennis lesson	yesterday. two days / weeks ago. last week / month.	The past tense ending of regular verbs is -ed. For irregular verbs, see the list below.
He / She We They	**had** didn't have			

	Yes / No questions	**Answers**
With *be*	Were you in class today?	Yes, I was. / No, I wasn't.
With other verbs	Did you pass the test?	Yes, I did. / No, I didn't.
	***Wh-* questions**	**Answers**
With *be*	Where were you last night?	(I was) at my friend's house.
With other verbs	When did you meet your girlfriend?	(We met) last year.

Regular Past Tense Verbs				Irregular Past Tense Verbs			
Base form	**Past tense**	**Base form**	**Past tense**	**Base form**	**Past tense**	**Base form**	**Past tense**
change	changed	pass	passed	be	was / were	know	knew
die	died	play	played	come	came	make	made
enter	entered	prepare	prepared	do	did	meet	met
finish	finished	practice	practiced	eat	ate	read	read
graduate	graduated	study	studied	give	gave	run	ran
help	helped	talk	talked	get	got	take	took
live	lived	travel	traveled	go	went	think	thought
marry	married	use	used	have	had	win	won
move	moved	work	worked	keep	kept	write	wrote

A Read about Diego's experience. Complete the sentences with the correct simple past tense forms of the verbs in parentheses.

In high school, I (1. study) _____ a lot and got good grades. But the first time I (2. take) _____ the university entrance exam, I (3. fail) _____. That (4. be) _____ hard. To prepare for the next exam, I (5. go) _____ to a test prep center. Two good things (6. happen) _____ there: I (7. meet) _____ my girlfriend in the class. And the next time I (8. take) _____ the entrance exam, I (9. pass) _____ it!

B Write six past tense questions about Diego. Then answer them on a separate piece of paper.

1. Was Diego a good student in high school? _____   4. _____

2. _____   5 _____

3. _____   6. _____

C Write sentences about things you did or didn't do yesterday. Use the verb phrases provided.

1. go to school   *I didn't go to school yesterday. I was sick.*

2. study for a test   _____

3. do homework   _____

4. practice English   _____

> Did you go to school yesterday?
>
> No, I didn't.
>
> Why not? What did you do?
>
> I stayed home. I was sick.

D 🔁 Ask a partner *Yes / No* questions to learn his or her answers in **C**. Then ask a follow-up *Wh-* question.

UNIT **2** LET'S EAT!

LESSON A

The Comparative Form of Adjectives	
This restaurant is **bigger than** that one.	Use the comparative form of an adjective to compare two things.
Your cooking is **better than** my mom's. My cold is **worse** today **than** it was yesterday.	The comparative of *good* is *better*. The comparative of *bad* is *worse*.
I'm tall, but Milo is **taller**.	Sometimes, you can use the comparative form without *than*.

One syllable	sweet → sweet**er**	Add *-er* to many one-syllable adjectives.
	large → large**r**	Add *-r* if the adjective ends in *-e*.
	big → big**ger**	Double the final consonant and add *-er* if the adjective ends in a vowel + consonant.
Two syllables	simple → simple**r** quiet → quiet**er**	Add *-r* or *-er* to two-syllable adjectives that end in an unstressed syllable.
	spicy → spic**ier**	Change the final *-y* to *-ier* if the adjective ends in *-y*.
	crowded → **more** crowded famous → **more** famous	Add *more* to other adjectives, especially those ending in *-ing*, *-ed*, *-ous*, or *-ful*.
Three syllables	relaxing → **more** relaxing delicious → **more** delicious	Add *more* to all adjectives with three or more syllables.

A Write the comparative form of the adjectives.

1. mild   _____
2. tasty   _____
3. popular   _____
4. hungry   _____
5. bad   _____

6. big   _____
7. good   _____
8. comfortable   _____
9. nice   _____
10. expensive   _____

B Read the facts. Then make a sentence using the comparative followed by *than*.

> Use *than* after the comparative when the two things being compared are mentioned in the same sentence: *The popcorn is saltier than the pretzels.*

A can of regular cola has 44 grams of sugar.

A can of diet cola has 0 grams of sugar.

1. (sweet) _____

Some people like baked chicken.

Everyone loves grilled chicken.

2. (popular) _____

Korean dishes are very spicy.

English dishes are not so spicy.

3. (spicy) _____

The streets in the village are empty.

There are a lot of cars on the streets in the city.

4. (busy) _____

It costs $30 to eat at the French restaurant.

It costs $10 to eat at the coffee shop.

5. (expensive) _____

LESSON B

The Superlative Form of Adjectives	
It's **the oldest** restaurant in Paris. (= The other restaurants are not as old.)	Use the superlative form of an adjective to compare something to an entire group.
It's **one of the oldest** restaurants in Paris. (= It's one of many old restaurants in Paris.)	Use *one of...* to show that something or someone is part of a group.
Mario's has **the best** pizza in the city. It was **the worst** movie of the year.	The superlative of *good* is *the best*. The superlative of *bad* is *the worst*.

One syllable	sweet → **the** sweet**est** large → **the** large**st**	Add *the* and *-est* or *-st* to many one-syllable adjectives.
Two syllables	quiet → **the** quiet**est** simple → **the** simpl**est**	Add *the* and *-est* or *-st* to two-syllable adjectives that end in an unstressed syllable.
	spicy → **the** spic**iest**	Add *the* and change the final *-y* to *-iest* if the adjective ends in *-y*.
	crowded → **the most** crowded famous → **the most** famous	Add *the most* to other adjectives, especially those ending in *-ing*, *-ed*, *-ous*, or *-ful*.
Three syllables	relaxing → **the most** relaxing delicious → **the most** delicious	Add *the most* to all adjectives with three or more syllables.

A Write the superlative form of the adjectives.

1. cheap _____
2. healthy _____
3. nervous _____
4. friendly _____
5. bad _____

6. unusual _____
7. good _____
8. helpful _____
9. tasty _____
10. expensive _____

B Complete the questions with the superlative form of the adjectives in parentheses.

1. Who is _____ (healthy) person in your family?
2. What is _____ (expensive) restaurant in your city?
3. What is _____ (good) food to eat when you're sick?
4. Who is _____ (popular) celebrity chef today?
5. What is _____ (bad) tasting food or drink?
6. What is _____ (hard) food or drink to eliminate from your diet?

C 🗨 Take turns asking and answering the questions in **B** with a partner.

UNIT **3** MYSTERIES

LESSON A

Stative Verbs
Stative verbs describe states and feelings (not actions).

agree	belong	hate	like	mind	prefer
appear	dislike	hear	love	need	seem
believe	doubt	know	mean	own	want

Usually, they are not used in the present continuous tense.	
He **seems** like a nice guy.	~~He is seeming like a nice guy.~~

Some stative verbs, however, can be used in the continuous. When used this way, their meaning changes.	
Do you **think** he's lucky? (*think* = believe) He **looks** happy. (*look* = appear)	I'm **thinking** about it. (*think* = consider) Who **is looking** in the window? (*look* = direct eyes toward)
She **has** a lucky object. (*has* = own; possess)	They're **having** coffee. (*have* = drink) **Are** you **having** fun? (*have* = experience)
I can't **see** without my glasses. (*see* = view with eyes) I **see** what you mean. (*see* = understand)	I'm **seeing** her tomorrow. (*see* = meet)

When you ask about how someone feels, you can use either form with no change in meaning.	
How do you **feel**?	How **are** you **feeling**?

A Circle the correct answer to complete each sentence. (In one case, both answers are possible.)

1. I bet that lucky people have / are having more friends.

2. Do you think / Are you thinking some people are just luckier in life?

3. Lucky charms seem / are seeming to really work.

4. I think / I'm thinking about this statement: It's better to be lucky than smart.

5. I doubt / I'm doubting it's a fact.

6. I hear / I'm hearing that Professor Wiseman is a well-known psychologist.

7. It looks / is looking like Amy called me at 2:00.

8. A: Do you belong / Are you belonging to the International Student Club?

   B: Yes. Do you know / Are you knowing that we have / we're having a party next week?

9. A: How do you feel? / How are you feeling?

   B: I have / I'm having a cold.

10. I see / I'm seeing my best friend tomorrow. We have / We're having lunch together.

LESSON B

Modals of Present Possibility			
Subject	**Modal**	**Main verb**	
The Loch Ness Monster	**may / might / could**	be	real. Maybe it's a large animal.
	can't		real. There are no sea monsters.

You can use *may*, *might*, and *could* to say something is possible in the present tense.
Use *can't* to say something is impossible.
You can use *may* or *might* with *not*: **He might / may not** speak French.
Do not use *could* with *not* for present possibility.

Questions and Short Answers		
With *be*	Is the Loch Ness Monster real?	It **may / might / could** be.
With other verbs	Does the full moon affect us?	It **may / might / could**.

A Complete the dialogs with a modal and a verb if needed.

1. A: How old is Karen?

   B: I don't know. She _____ 35.

   C: She _____ be 35. She graduated from college in 1980.

2. A: Do ghosts exist?

   B: They _____. No one knows for sure.

3. A: Where's Lauren?

   B: I'm not sure. She _____ with Lin. They always hang out together after school.

   A: She _____ be with Lin. Lin is on vacation.

4. A: Are the Nazca Lines a type of calendar?

   B: They _____. It's one possible explanation.

B Read each situation. Write two possible explanations for each one on a piece of paper.

1. Your friend isn't answering her phone.

2. You received a mysterious package in the mail.

3. The teacher isn't here today.

4. A new student in class is very quiet.

C 🔄 Work with a partner. Follow the steps below.

1. **Student A:** Tell your partner one situation in **B**.

2. **Student B:** Give a possible reason, using one of your sentences in **B**.

3. **Student A:** Answer with a negative modal.

4. **Student B:** Give your second idea.

5. Change roles and repeat steps 1–4. Do this until you talk about all the situations in **B**.

> My friend isn't answering her phone.

> Her phone might be off.

> It can't be. She called me two minutes ago.

> Oh, then she may be...

UNIT **4**　TRENDS

LESSON A

Quantity Expressions with Specific Nouns				
Quantity word	*of*	**Determiner***	**Plural count noun**	
All **Most** **A lot** **Half** **Some** **None**	of	my	friends	live at home.
		Pronoun		
		them		

Use these quantity expressions to talk about amounts with **specific** nouns.

They can also be used with noncount nouns: *Half of my <u>homework</u> is finished.*

The word *of* is optional after *all* when it is followed by a determiner and a noun: *All (of) my friends live at home.*

*A determiner is a small word like *the, that,* or *my.*

Quantity Expressions with General Nouns		
Quantity word	**Plural count noun**	
All **Most** **A lot of** **Some**	students	study hard.

100% ⬆ all
most
a lot
half
⬇ some
0% none

Use *all, most, a lot of,* and *some* followed by a noun to make **general** statements about people or things everywhere.

These expressions can also be used with noncount nouns: *Most water is clean.*

A Complete the sentences with the correct word(s). Some items may have more than one correct answer.

1. Some / Some of people want to be happy in life.
2. Most / Most of my friends speak English, but none / none of them speak it at home.
3. Some / Some of students live with their families because it's cheaper.
4. Half / Half of our neighbors have children. A couple / couple of them have pets, too.
5. All / All of parents want their children to do well in school.
6. All / All of the instructors at my school are really strict.

B Do you agree with the sentences in **A**? Rewrite them by changing the quantity words as necessary.

LESSON B

Giving Advice with *could*, *should*, *ought to*, and *had better*	
You **could** wear a dress to the party. You **could** wear the blue dress or the black one.	Use *could* to make a suggestion or give advice. It is often used to offer two or more choices.
You **should / ought to** wear a formal suit to the job interview. You **shouldn't** wear jeans. They're too casual.	Use *should* or *ought to* to give advice. Both are stronger than *could*. Use *shouldn't* in the negative.
You**'d better** wear a coat. It's going to rain. We**'d better not** drive to the concert. It will be hard to park.	Use *had better (not)* to give strong advice. It sounds like a warning or order. Use the contracted form (*you'd better*) in speaking.

Use *could*, *should*, *ought to*, or *had better* to give advice about something in the present or the near future.
These are all followed by the <u>base form</u> of a verb: *You could / should / ought to / had better <u>wear</u> a suit.*

A Complete the conversations with the expressions in the boxes. Use each expression only once.

shouldn't	could	ought to

A: I don't know what to wear to the party tonight.

B: You (1.) _____ wear your new skinny jeans or black pants.

A: It's a formal dinner party.

B: Oh, then you (2.) _____ wear jeans. They're too casual. You definitely (3.) _____ wear the black pants.

A: I still don't understand this grammar.

could	had better not	had better

B: You (4.) _____ get some help. The test is on Thursday.

A: Maybe I (5.) _____ take the test on Friday. That would give me extra time.

B: Well, talk to the teacher, but you (6.) _____ delay. There's not much time!

NOTES